Critical Multicultural
Social Work

Also Available from Lyceum Books, Inc.

Critical Multicultural Social Work

JOSE SISNEROS
NEW MEXICO HIGHLANDS UNIVERSITY

CATHERINE STAKEMAN
NATIONAL ASSOCIATION OF SOCIAL WORKERS

MILDRED C. JOYNER
WEST CHESTER UNIVERSITY

CATHRYNE L. SCHMITZ
UNIVERSITY OF NORTH CAROLINA AT GREENSBORO

LYCEUM
BOOKS, INC.

Chicago, Illinois

© Lyceum Books, Inc., 2008

Published by

LYCEUM BOOKS, INC.
5758 S. Blackstone Ave.
Chicago, Illinois 60637
773+643-1903 (Fax)
773+643-1902 (Phone)
lyceum@lyceumbooks.com
http://www.lyceumbooks.com

6 5 4 3 2 1   08 09 10 11

ISBN 978-1-933478-14-2

Library of Congress Cataloging-in-Publication Data

Critical multicultural social work / Jose Sisneros . . . [et al.].
    p. cm.
  Includes bibliographical references and index.
  ISBN 978-1-933478-14-2
  1. Social work with minorities. 2. Social work with gays. 3. Social work with
people with disabilites. I. Sisneros, Jose.
  HV3176.C75   2008
  361.3—dc22
                                                    2008002750

This book is dedicated to those who are inheriting our past and charged with creating our future. We hope this book will support the process of healing and growth so our children and grandchildren inherit a kinder world.

Contents

Boxes, Tables, and Figures

About the Authors

Jose A. Sisneros, LISW, PhD, is associate professor at New Mexico Highlands University. He received his MSW from Arizona State University, and his PhD from the University of Denver. He teaches at the graduate and undergraduate levels, specializing in diversity courses. He also teaches a course for the bilingual program titled "Social Development in Mexico and in Latino/a Immigrant Communities in the United States." He taught previously at the University of Denver, where he was instrumental in the development of a course on multiculturalism in social work and was the architect and coordinator for the Latino/Latina certificate program. Professor Sisneros has thirty-two years of practice experience as a social worker. He has worked in community mental health settings, in which he held direct practice and administrative positions. Much of his experience has been working with Latino/Latina clients and in programs for Latinos and Latinas. His last community position was as clinical director at Servicios De La Raza, a specialty clinic serving the Latino community in Denver, Colorado. He is actively engaged in research and scholarship on diversity, Latino families, pedagogy, and multiculturalism.

Catherine Stakeman, LCSW, MSW, DSW, is currently the executive director of the NASW Maine Chapter and was formally an assistant professor at the University of Southern Maine School of Social Work, where she developed and taught courses on diversity for seven years. She has an MSW from Boston College, and a DSW from Catholic University in Washington, D.C. She spent many years as a social work practitioner, working mostly with children, youths, and families, and has taught in South Africa. Her scholarship focuses on diversity and multiculturalism at the local and global levels. She has coauthored several articles on multiculturalism and global issues and has presented on multicultural issues at numerous conferences and workshops.

Mildred C. Joyner, MSW, LCSW, BCD, is professor of social work and director/chairperson of the Undergraduate Social Work Program at West Chester University in West Chester, Pennsylvania. Her passion for social justice and empowerment of all people developed while she pursued her MSW at Howard University School of Social Work in Washington, D.C. Over the last twenty-five years she has served as a diversity consultant and expert speaker on the topic of race relations for higher, secondary, and elementary education, and for business and human service agencies. Over the last five years she has presented at over sixty national, state, and local conferences focusing on the eradication of "isms." As a part of her commitment to change, she serves as the vice president/treasurer of the Council on Social Work Education; the chairperson of the Board for Living Beyond Breast Cancer in Ardmore, Pennsylvania; and a bank director for DNB First in Downingtown, Pennsylvania. She has held positions as the president of the Association of Baccalaureate Social Work Program Directors and secretary of the Institute for the Advancement of Social Work Research.

Cathryne L. Schmitz, ACSW, PhD, is professor and chairperson/director of the Department of Social Work at the University of North Carolina at Greensboro. She received her MSW from the University of Washington, and her PhD in social work from the Ohio State University. She has extensive experience in multicultural multidisciplinary social work practice, leadership, administration, and education. She has developed curricula focused on critical multiculturalism and taught a social work course that involved taking students to Mexico to study global relations. Much of her scholarship focuses on multicultural relationships, the dismantling of oppression, poverty and its impact, leadership, and interdisciplinary education and practice. Professionally, she maintains interests in knowledge building and evaluation of multidisciplinary service delivery and administrative practice with different populations. Her commitment to dismantling oppression and empowering marginalized groups is also reflected through her service on committees for the Council on Social Work Education and the Association of Baccalaureate Social Work Program Directors. She is a coeditor of *Diversity in Single-Parent Families: Working From Strength* and *Child Labor: A Global View* and has authored numerous articles. She recently completed a study with adults who grew up in families with a gay or lesbian parent.

Preface

Over the past decade, the major organizations representing social workers have demonstrated a firm commitment to multicultural social work. In 2001, citing the significant growth of populations of color in the United States between 1990 and 2000, the National Association of Social Workers published the *Standards for Cultural Competence in Social Work Practice.* The same year, the Council on Social Work Education published its *Educational Policy and Accreditation Standards,* in which it outlines its commitment to nondiscrimination and addresses the need to integrate curriculum on diversity, populations at risk, and social and economic justice. Despite these advances, social work education has not yet embraced an explicit educational framework that includes both diversity and oppression (Schmitz et al., 2001; Van Soest, Canon, & Grant, 2000).

This book aims to address the lack of such a framework by approaching diversity content from a critical multicultural perspective. Combined, the authors have more than 116 years of experience as social work practitioners and educators. We are fueled by the knowledge that the quality of our children's and grandchildren's lives is dependent upon our ability to heal the wounds and dismantle the systems of oppression. We are also fueled by our passion for advancing the social work profession. The interactive process of teaching is a journey. This journey has changed us. We have taught, written, presented, and discussed critical multiculturalism in multiple contexts. We have taught single-group courses on topics such as social work practice with Latinos and Latinas, African Americans, and women. We have taught and practiced social work in the United States, Mexico, and South Africa. We bring multiple views on diversity and multiculturalism. In addition, we represent a variety of races and ethnicities, genders, and sexual orientations. We have all been active in developing curricula and teaching courses on diversity, and we have been frustrated by the fact that a textbook to help educators prepare incoming students for critical multicultural practice does not exist.

There are many books on cross-cultural practice and cultural competence. Nothing exists, however, to prepare social workers for the exploration of multicultural practice from a critical perspective. The study of multiculturalism, anti-oppression work, and social justice practice is in its infancy. This book engages readers in a process of personal reflection and knowledge building. After a discussion of oppression and basic theoretical framework for evaluating multiple issues of diversity and unequal access to power are presented in the first chapter, the focus shifts to self-reflection. In chapters 3, 4, and 5, specific oppressed groups are examined, analyzed, and deconstructed and explored within a critical multicultural context, which acknowledges the structural and power dynamics of oppression and examines the specific mechanisms of oppression of each group; issues of class and economics are interwoven.

In chapter 6 the complexity of intersections between race/ethnicity; gender, sex, and sexual orientation; and disabilities are analyzed. Readers are challenged to think critically about these dimensions and how they are intersected by issues of class. The metaphor of a web is used to explore the holistic complexity of the intersection of oppression; it allows us to acknowledge that multiple oppressions are not simply additive in their effect. Chapter 7 introduces readers to the practice arenas in which these issues most frequently surface and the tenets of critical multiculturalism can be applied. Throughout the text, opportunities for self-reflection are interspersed with content on multiculturalism, power, and the complexity of oppression.

We bring these issues to life through the use of case examples and a process that engages the reader in questioning hidden assumptions. The concerns, issues, and fears commonly raised by students as they begin to study diversity and oppression are discussed. History is viewed as if through the multiple lenses of a kaleidoscope, and readers are encouraged to recognize the many worldviews that produce these stories. This framework prepares the reader to undertake a critical analysis of oppression and institutional injustices, the impact of privilege, and processes for achieving wide-reaching change.

Because the issues and their contexts are always changing, each journey through this book will be different. Readers will examine these issues through their own lens, which is grounded in each individual's unique culture, family, community, and history. Each reader's engagement will also be based in her or his national origin and age or life stage. We wish you a challenging, interesting, and ultimately enjoyable journey.

Acknowledgments

We want to thank our spouses, partners, children, grandchildren, and other family members for inspiring and supporting us in our work. Our love for them reminds us that we want to create spaces of hope. There are also many friends and colleagues who have joined us along the way to help us learn, grow, and write. Without their help, this book would not have been possible. We want to give special thanks to Lacey Sloan, B.J. Bryson, Elizabeth KimJin Traver, and Gina McCaskill for their insightful contributions.

Chapter 1

Critical Multiculturalism and Oppression

An injustice anywhere is a threat to justice everywhere.

Martin Luther King Jr., "Letter from a Birmingham Jail"

This first chapter challenges the reader to think about the lens she or he uses to view the history, group relationships, and political discourse of the United States. This process establishes a framework for the exploration of issues of multiculturalism. Multiple models and theoretical perspectives with a focus on critical multiculturalism and the mechanisms of oppression are introduced as the portal for investigation.

U.S. history is really a patchwork of overlapping stories, perspectives, and worldviews. The history and perspectives presented here go beyond what is traditionally taught. The voices of those who have been silenced and oppressed are brought forward. By expanding perspectives and reframing ideas, we find places where histories overlap. As some groups have experienced privilege, other groups have experienced oppression.

The complex knowledge-building process in which we are challenged to engage as we relearn history can trigger multiple responses. The dominant group whose story is told in the United States is that of the healthy and economically privileged white heterosexual male. Recasting and sharing that story can feel unsettling and can lead to resistance and disbelief. Taking an expanded view of history to note the contributions of people of color, women, people with disabilities, and gay, lesbian, bisexual, and transgender communities be can both freeing and maddening for members of these groups. Responses such as "Where was I before? Why was I negated?" can surface (see box 1.1).

Box 1.1   What I Learned in the Conversation

Professor: Thank you for coming back to talk with this class. What would you tell this group to keep in mind as they explore issues of oppression and diversity?

Yolanda: First, stay with the conversation, even when you are angry and want to reject everything you hear.

Tom: I agree. I remember how angry I was. In my head, I said, "This professor is so prejudiced. She doesn't care about what I've been through. She only wants to get her political agenda across." I kept thinking, "Why all the talk about racism?" I did not see it as a problem. After all, I believed that civil rights had changed the way we as a society viewed black Americans, right? Why the talk about heterosexism? The only "ism" that I felt needed to be discussed was ableism. All the others I just did not consider an issue at all.

Yolanda: My deepest frustration in the beginning was that students were unwilling to talk. On the other hand, there was Tom. I must admit that at the beginning of the class, I wanted to strangle him; however, I can now appreciate where he was coming from because of his honesty. My hope is that as social work students, you will continue to talk about racism and all the other "isms" as well and how they all intersect.

Tom: When I first heard Yolanda speak about her experience, I thought that she was exaggerating. I felt that she fit the profile of an angry black woman. I felt everything about her and everything she said was just too radical. Looking back, however, I realize that I simply did not understand her; I was really wrong. It is important for students to keep an open mind. Be careful not to judge.

Yolanda: I would like to add to that, Tom. It is also important that students do not take anything said as a personal attack on them. If someone decides to open up about her experience as a black female in a white society, do not take offense; do not shut down. Listen.

Tom: As a white male from an impoverished and isolated rural community, I can tell you that as you begin this course, you will feel as though you have a target on your back. Just hang in there and remember what Yolanda said about not taking things personally. Instead, think about how you can make a difference.

Yolanda: I was afraid to talk at the beginning of the class because I was concerned that other students simply would not understand. As a woman of color, I was moved to tears by this class. It was painful, but I feel that I have grown because of it. It was extremely helpful that the professor was there facilitating and helping us work through our issues.

Tom: You are not alone, Yolanda. Most of the discussions had me squirming in my seat. I felt very uncomfortable when I learned about white privilege. I felt guilty, although not responsible, just guilty for not recognizing and acknowledging the benefits of my whiteness, my gender, and my heterosexuality—my privilege.

Yolanda: It was very lonely those first couple of weeks. I felt that I did not have an ally in the room. The more I spoke up, the more isolated I felt. Then, one by one, other students finally began to speak up. I felt particularly close to the white lesbian students because I felt that they really understood. For the most part, I believe that they were saying, "Hey, wait a minute, this is our struggle too. Let's tear things down. Let's do things differently going forward. How can we change this white male heterosexist patriarchy together?"

Tom: Some people are born to fight and others are not. It is important that everyone step out of their comfort zone and choose a battle. Whether you choose racism, sexism, homophobia, whatever, work to change something in your own way. It can be quiet. It can be loud.

Yolanda: Tom, I disagree with you there. I do not understand why we cannot work simultaneously on the "isms." Why just one battle?

Tom: You are right. I realize that they do not occur in a vacuum. What I meant was that we should strive for change. I love to read and watch the news. Eventually, I began to see how everything we discussed in class was intersecting with what I was reading and seeing in the news and it was all happening simultaneously. Although the intersections were not always obvious, they were there and I could see them. Now, I view the world and the news from an entirely different perspective. We are all connected and so are the issues.

It is only through a discussion of difference and an expanded view of history that acknowledges that the oppression of some brings privilege for others that we can move toward change. In investigating these issues, we entertain the possibility described by bell hooks (1995) in her discussion of the beloved community. Her vision is one of love; it is one of creating community by embracing difference. We can only create change and a space in which to live together through the discussion of our differences. In coming together, exploring difference, and working against oppression in our daily lives, we create community and welcome the possibility of change.

So, explore the expanded multicultural story of the United States. Challenge existing perceptions, embrace discomfort, and accept that difference exists. Explore the issues that engender resistance and discomfort. A patchwork of the multiple intertwined stories emerges. This history is so much richer than could have been imagined.

Theories and Concepts of Structure, Diversity, and Inequality

There are many theories and models that can be used to examine the issues and concepts of diversity, multiculturalism, and inequality in the United States. The concept of *critical multiculturalism* provides the framework for analysis in this book. It is a concept that allows us to move beyond the goal of learning about and appreciating diversity to engage in an exploration of the multiple and complex power relations of difference and the mechanisms of oppression that operate in society. The examination of multiculturalism and oppression from a critical perspective involves an analysis of the systems that maintain and perpetuate inequality, with the presumption of a commitment to egalitarianism through action.

Structural theories of social stratification argue that existing systems of stratification (the placement of different groups in society) are universal, functional, and necessary to the social order (Davis, Moore, & Tumin, 2006; Tumin,

1953).These theories focus on class and individual inequality (Meyer, 1994). Inequality is justified, and group inequalities are ignored. According to those with power and privilege, resources are scarce and limited and must be won by those with talent. While structural role theory provides a basic structure for understanding expectations based on social status and class, it is limiting and overly prescriptive regarding the social world (Turner, 1991).This theory examines systems of oppression, roles, motivation, and access to resources within the context of social structure, rather than as mechanisms that establish and maintain collective inequality. Meyer (1994) asserts that "The inattention to collective and cultural aspects of stratification has been a substantial limitation in the field" (p. 731).The study of social stratification and the "broad consequences of social differentiation and inequality for individuals and social systems" raises questions of greater significance (Baron, Grusky, & Treiman, 1996, p. 360).Tumin (1953) contends that systems of social inequality are limiting and alienating and challenges the basic assumptions of theories that support the necessity of social inequality on the grounds that there is no evidence to support the notion that social equality is impossible.

Expanded notions of stratification take into account the analysis of macro systems.They acknowledge that access to resources is controlled by the elite, those in positions of privilege (Tumin, 1953). Systems benefit some groups while withholding resources from others. Being in a position of privilege—for example, having parents who can support higher education—increases one's opportunities.They also recognize that as a result of the structural limitations imposed on historically oppressed groups, the discourse reflects little awareness of their talent and skills.The move beyond theories of rigid roles and the vision of individuals as actors in a play to ones that assess systems of oppression and view individuals and communities as potential agents of change broadens one's perspective. Possibilities for change then emerge. Anthias (2001) argues "that it is necessary to develop an analysis which is able to understand unequal *social outcomes*" (p. 387).

Likewise, the study of diversity, as it is commonly practiced in social work, can be narrow and limiting. Students often learn about different cultures by reading literature from marginalized groups and participating in bridging activities, which introduce students to other cultures through what Kanpol (1997) calls the four F's—fairs, food, festivals, and folktales—or as Banks (1997) said, "teepees and chitlins." This approach has some value but is not sufficient. Although difference is acknowledged, the difficult issues of power and domination are not addressed.

Multiculturalism acknowledges the heterogeneity of difference and that power, domination, and socioeconomic class shape structures and interactions. Multiculturalism, a concept originating in Canada, is a relatively new notion and has many definitions (Glazer, 1997). Several models of multiculturalism exist (see table 1.1; see Kincheloe & Steinberg, 1997, for a thorough discussion). Conservative, liberal, and pluralist definitions of multiculturalism rationalize

TABLE 1.1 The Five Forms of Multiculturalism

Form of Multiculturalism	Definition
Conservative	• Focuses on white Western patriarchal culture • Believes the Western system is the best and should be imposed on others • Believes in economic imperialism, or control of the economies of less powerful nations by more powerful nations • Places blame for marginalization on individuals or their community • Denies the existence of mechanisms of oppression • Ignores issues regarding access to power
Liberal	• Denies the fact that different groups have different levels of access to resources and opportunities • Subscribes to a philosophy of "color blindness," which makes racial minorities invisible • Ignores class and gender differences • Views white male standards/values as the ideal • Believes that assimilation is the answer
Pluralist	• Focuses on difference, separate but equal • Only recognizes safe and controllable dimensions of difference • Shares shortcomings of liberal multiculturalism • Values the coexistence of people from different cultures • Believes that anyone can make it by working hard • Confuses psychological affirmation with political empowerment • Does not address socioeconomic status/structural inequality • Celebrates difference while ignoring powerlessness, violence, and poverty
Left-essentialist	• Focuses on differences as an essential piece of identity • Fails to acknowledge difference within identity groups • Believes that authenticity transcends history, social context, and power • Has a tendency to romanticize difference • Rejects biological basis for differences but downplays the impact of history • Believes only oppressed people can possess moral authority to speak about oppression • Assumes cultures are equal and there is no bias
Critical	• Focuses on emancipation • Views identity formation as socially constructed and constantly shifting • Believes that self-reflection promotes changes of perspective • Makes no pretense of neutrality • Works to expose processes that privilege the affluent and undermine the poor • Is dedicated to egalitarianism and elimination of human suffering

TABLE 1.1   The Five Forms of Multiculturalism—(*continued*)

Form of Multiculturalism	Definition
	• Sees class as a central concern as it interacts with race, gender, and other axes of power • Is concerned with the contextualization of inequalities and how power has operated historically • Acknowledges that there are as many differences within cultural groups as there are between them • Acknowledges that power relations shape our consciousness • Acknowledges that ideological inscriptions become imprinted on our subjectivity • Recognizes that culture reproduces power relations and constructs experiences that preserve the privilege of white supremacy, patriarchy, class elitism, and other oppressive forces • Seeks to understand the power of difference when conceptualized within the larger concerns of social justice

Source: Adapted from Kincheloe, J., & Steinberg, S. R. (1997). *Changing multiculturalism.* Philadelphia, PA: Open University Press.

behavior, preserve privilege, and conceal the many ways in which power hierarchies protect ideology and social order. According to left-essentialist multiculturalism, one form of oppression takes precedence over all other kinds; that is, single-identity groups work for themselves in competition with other groups, not in coalitions. For example, the early women's movement failed to address issues of race, class, and sexual orientation. Similarly, the civil rights movement did not address issues of gender, class, and sexual orientation.

Critical multiculturalism builds from the work of many theorists, including Freire and the Frankfurt school of critical theory. The concept enables us to move beyond the recognition of distinct cultures and places an emphasis on understanding oppression in juxtaposition to privilege (Fuller, 2000). A critical multicultural education focuses specifically on raising the consciousness of social groups that are or have been oppressed and the systems that foster that oppression. Critical consciousness—the ability to question one's history and social position for the purpose of confronting inequality—and sensitivity provide a base for the development of critical thinking.

Critical thinking involves an examination that looks beyond the immediate information presented. Through analytical exploration, assessment, integration, and synthesis, the deeper political, social, and economic ramifications of the information are considered. The learner engages in a process that weaves together self-reflection, knowledge building, and an understanding of the role power plays in framing and maintaining relationships (Giroux, 1997). Neither personal experience nor politics can be ignored. Freire (1991) and Giroux (1993) highlight the importance of drawing on self-knowledge in building cultural literacy and the ability to think critically. Critical analysis embraces the complexity of conceptualizing difference and the layers of systemic inequality. Critical thinking thus provides the necessary springboard for action, emancipation, and social change. "An individual who has gained . . . a consciousness [of him- or herself] understands how and why his or her political opinions, socio-economic class, role, religious beliefs, gender role and racial self-image are shaped by dominant perspectives" (Kincheloe & Steinberg, 1997, p. 23).

Critical multicultural social work requires the ability to conceptualize more than one difference at a time because there are as many differences within cultural groups as there are between them (Kincheloe & Steinberg, 1997). It is not just about critically analyzing, but also about taking action to ensure social and economic justice are attainable for everyone. In the movement toward equality, critical multiculturalists work to expose the subtle and often hidden processes that sustain and perpetuate the privilege of certain groups and the processes that undermine the efforts of groups marginalized by class, race, gender and sex, sexual orientation, and ability status.

The critical multicultural perspective builds from a variety of social theories that challenge the idea that knowledge is objective and stresses the historical context in which all knowledge is based (critical theory), challenge the idea that social structures are natural and understand reality to be subjective and constructed through individual interactions (social constructivist theory), and seek to understand and challenge oppression and acknowledge that oppression is learned and privilege is conferred and maintained by social structures (anti-oppression theory). Culture cannot be simplified, nor can it be separated from race and the other dimensions of the multicultural spectrum. Our construction of reality is determined by scripts (i.e., messages) learned from places such as family, school, and the media and can therefore be re-scripted as we open up a space to dialogue with others and understand their perceptions of reality. Each day, we re-create our reality socially, constructing our history and our future as we construct our experience each moment. Our beliefs and fears are also socially constructed (Loseke & Best, 2003).

Mechanisms of Oppression

The mechanisms of oppression are complex. Oppression is pervasive, restricting, and hierarchical, affecting society at both the individual and systemic levels (Bell, 1997). Oppression silences the voices of marginalized people and their allies. People often suffer disadvantage and injustice "not because of a tyrannical power coerces them, but because of the everyday practices of a well-intentioned liberal society" (Young, 1990, p. 41). Both conscious assumptions and discrimination as well as unconscious attitudes and behaviors contribute to the system of oppression (Bell, 1997).

Subordinate groups are denied opportunities to participate fully in society and do not have the rights of the dominant group. They are assigned second-class citizenship not because of individual merit or failures, but because of their membership in a category. Oppression systematically reduces, molds, and immobilizes individual members of a group or category. Oppression is interactive and qualitative rather than quantitative, occurring when individuals and groups are blocked from opportunities for self-development (Weinman, 1984). By definition, structural arrangements favor a dominant (privileged) group over a subordinate group (Mullaly, 2002). When a multiplicity of oppressions, which are mutually reinforcing and additive, intersect at multiple sites, they create new oppressions at their juncture. For instance, a Latina may experience at least three forms of oppression: oppression as a woman, oppression as a person of color, and oppression as a woman of color. As noted by Pharr (2000), "It is virtually impossible to view one oppression, such as sexism or homophobia, in isolation because they are all connected: sexism, racism, homophobia, classism, ableism, anti-Semitism, ageism. They are linked by a common origin—economic power and control—and by common methods of limiting, controlling and destroying lives. There is no hierarchy of oppressions. Each is terrible and destructive. To eliminate one oppression successfully, a movement has to include work to eliminate them all or else success will always be limited and incomplete" (p. 53). Systems of oppression affect each one of us, whether we are part of a privileged group or part of a subordinate group. Most of us experience positions of privilege in some parts of our lives while experiencing oppression in other areas.

Young's (1990) conceptualization of the five faces of oppression—exploitation, marginalization, powerlessness, cultural imperialism, and violence—offers a tool for understanding the types of oppression that groups experience (see table 1.2). Exploitation refers to those social processes whereby the dominant group accumulates and maintains status, power, and assets from the energy and labor expended by subordinate groups (Mullaly, 2002). Marginalization is the expulsion of whole groups of people from mainstream society that occurs when dominant groups are defined as the norm; this denies those not in dominant or privileged groups the opportunity to participate in society in useful and meaningful ways. This powerlessness results in the placement of limitations on the development of one's capacities, a lack of decision-making power, and exposure to disrespectful treatment based on group membership and status. Cultural imperialism is the imposition of the dominant culture on other populations. Finally, violence and the threat of violence serve to keep marginalized groups stigmatized and intimidated.

The struggle against oppression is often met with violence by the oppressors, which results in the dehumanization of the oppressed (Freire, 1982). The oppressors also suffer from the "psychic and ethical violence" of oppression (Bell, 1997, p. 7). The process of oppression hurts both the oppressed and the oppressor (Bell, 1997; Freire, 1982).

Because oppression operates on three levels—individual, institutional, and cultural/societal—change must occur on multiple levels simultaneously (Hardiman & Jackson, 1997). The process of change begins with the development of critical consciousness and sensitivity. That consciousness and sensitivity must

TABLE 1.2   The Five Faces of Oppression

Face	Definition	Example
Exploitation	The products of the labor of one social group are transferred to benefit another group. Social rules defining work, who performs the work, the compensation for work, and the social process by which the results are appropriated operate to enact relations of power and inequality.	Migrant laborers, primarily people of color, harvest produce for low wages with few or no benefits. This keeps the cost of produce low.
Marginalization	Whole groups of people, the marginalized, are denied the opportunity to participate in social life and thus can be subjected to severe material deprivation and even extermination.	A building does not have the ramps and elevators that a person in a wheelchair needs to enter and get around.
Powerlessness	Marginalized groups lack of authority, status, and sense of self.	Single mothers receiving public assistance are treated with disrespect.
Cultural imperialism	The culture and experience of the dominant group is established as the norm. All others are judged by this standard of normalcy.	Relationships in nonwhite communities are judged by white middle-class norms and values.
Violence	Groups are subjected to physical violence, harassment, ridicule, intimidation, and stigmatization. Direct victimization results in intimidation and the constant fear that violence may occur solely on the basis of one's membership in or identification with the group.	Gay youths are often verbally harassed and physically threatened in their schools.

Source: Adapted from Young, I. M. (1990). *Justice and the politics of difference.* Princeton, NJ: Princeton University Press.

then be used to move to action (Freire, 1982; hooks, 1994). The process of bringing critical consciousness and sensitivity to meaningful practice is what Freire called praxis. Integral to the concept of praxis is the development of skills for critical analysis, which views "reality as process, as transformation, rather than as a static entity—thinking which does not separate itself from action" (Freire, 1982, p. 81).

Systems of oppression are maintained through practices that do not question "the assumptions and underlying institutional rules and the collective consequences of following those rules" (Young, 1990, p. 41). The challenge is for those who have been oppressed to resist persistent oppressive forces, regain their humanity, and create change without perpetuating similar power hierarchies and using tactics of oppression like those of the current oppressors. Of course, those who are in positions of power must join with the oppressed to restore the humanity of both the oppressed and the oppressor (Freire, 1982). The dismantling of oppression is a mission for everyone and, in particular, everyone in the social work profession.

Discourse of Division

The framing of diversity and multiculturalism as frightening and threatening creates alarm and ignites hostility. Since the so-called Contract with America in 1994, conservative pundits have aligned multiculturalism with anti-American ideals, and dialogue on political correctness has served to rally a backlash against discussion of the strengths of diversity. As a part of this backlash, language is being used in a way that silences critical analysis as well as debate. Liberal has become a "bad" word, framed to mean an individual or community without values. On the other hand, being conservative has been claimed to be synonymous with having the "right" and "good" values. As a result, conservatives might view themselves as having the right to control dialogue and silence disparate views. According to another perspective, however, a liberal is someone who tolerates and values differences, while a conservative is someone who insists that her or his views are the only correct ones.

The discourse of the neoconservative political right creates a climate of fear (Chernus, 2006). Most recently, stories of Middle Eastern terrorists, the sin of homosexuality, and the immigrant "other" have served to frighten and divide the country. Giroux (1994) has observed that in his book *The Death of the West,* Pat Buchanan, a major spokesperson for the political right, centers multiculturalism as a major threat to democracy and justice. Buchanan and others play on people's fears by blaming diversity and multiculturalism for all social and economic problems. People who feel vulnerable financially are led to believe that it is people of color, rather than an oppressive economic system, who are causing their economic struggles. As Thomas Friedman (2006) points out, the rate of societal change is increasing rapidly, and unless we are prepared to think critically about these changes, the process will continue to create fears that can easily be manipulated.

Too often, the mainstream media becomes a tool that is used to suppress change. Diversity is portrayed as unsettling and disruptive to the United States. This results in fearful responses to bilingual programs and affirmative action, cries to militarize the Mexican border, and calls for massive immigration sweeps. One of the arguments against affirmative action is that white men are now victims of "reverse discrimination." This argument, which Fiscuss (1992) refers to as the "innocent person's argument," suggests that affirmative action programs force employers to hire unqualified people of color and women instead of better-qualified white men. While these programs do not give people from oppressed groups preference, the loss of preference can feel like discrimination to historically privileged groups. As affirmative action programs attempt to reduce the preference given to privileged groups, individuals from privileged groups lose some of the preference that is built into institutionalized practices. The perception that affirmative action favors historically oppressed groups creates both fear and confusion. It is often difficult to recognize the inherent privilege of being white, male, and heterosexual. Questioning and disrupting institutional norms and assumptions often leaves us confused and anxious. The recognition of this led Freire (1982) to examine the role of education in the development of critical consciousness and sensitivity. Bringing assumptions that lead to the production and maintenance of the structures of domination and enforce oppression out into the open offers the possibility of the creation of alternative structures and the reorganization of social and political life.

Fortunately, social order is not a static given, but a fluid condition to be worked upon and changed (Freire, 1982). Social movements build from the cultivation of critical consciousness, and critical multicultural education can become a tool for change (Gil, 1998). The foundation of critical consciousness, which characterized early social movements, supports the unveiling of such assumptions. Assumptions underlying institutional rules, and the collective consequences of these rules, are embedded in unquestioned norms, habits, and symbols. "Systemic restraints on groups are not necessarily the result of a tyrant but rather structural. . . . [They are] the result of a few people's choices or policies" (Young, 1990, p. 41). Behaviors and attitudes that serve to preserve the oppression-privilege interchange are entrenched and hidden in the ordinariness of everyday life. "Societies became what they are through the actions, relations, and consciousness of their members, and they are reproduced through people's socialization and conformity to previously institutionalized patterns of actions, relations, and consciousness" (Gil, 1998, p. 57).

Multiple Threads to the Story

As we develop a critical consciousness, it becomes possible to recognize that as privilege is maintained, the assumption of normality of the privileged group is internalized. For instance, heterosexuality carries the unconscious assumption of normality. This assumption can be challenged as lesbian, gay, bisexual, and transgender individuals and allies speak out and confront prevailing assumptions of normality. Similarly, as we begin to understand that the dominant group constructs history, thereby defining normality, we can start to dispute such privilege.

The United States, from its beginning, has been challenged in its development as a multicultural society (Schmitz, Stakeman, & Sisneros, 2001; see Takaki, 1993, and Zinn, 2003, for a thorough history). The ongoing process of building this nation is complex; the nation is a fabric woven from many

countries, continents, and cultures. The pieces are jagged and do not fit together smoothly. These junctures cause a pain that has led to misunderstand-
ing, denial, anger, sadness, and confusion. In order to tell the story from a multicultural perspective, it is important to take the time to research the facts and
view history from various perspectives. This process requires both learning
and unlearning. Reexamining and embracing history in all its complexity helps
us understand the richness of the many groups and cultures living together in
the United States. This knowledge allows us to acknowledge and appreciate
the resiliency of all people.

Because history is framed from the point of view of the historians who
record and pass on information, the established history with which we are most
familiar was told from the perspective of males of western European descent,
primarily those of economic means. The resistance and resilience of Native
Americans, African Americans, Asian Americans, Latinos/Latinas, and the poor
and working class have been omitted or distorted (Schmitz et al., 2001; Takaki,
1993; Zinn, 2003). There is a gap in written history regarding women, people
with disabilities, and those labeled "other" by virtue of their sexual orientation,
gender identification, and religion. Only recently have we begun to hear history
from different perspectives.

When western Europeans arrived in North America, many indigenous cultures already had deep and settled roots. The newcomers, who came as adven-
turers, settlers, and indentured servants, most often misunderstood, overlooked,
disrespected, and ignored the integrity of these indigenous communities.
Treaties forced on Native Americans resulted in the transfer of land from indigenous communities to white settlers. The colonists were a diverse group as
well. They came from many countries, religions, cultures, and classes. Some had
great privilege and wealth; others experienced extreme poverty. Some came to
escape religious persecution; some were criminals who were sent to the so-
called New World. Within this mix were also many individuals and families from
a variety of African countries and cultures. Stripped of their humanity, many
were brought as indentured servants and slaves. Immigrants from the South
(Latin America) and the East (Asia) came later. Adding to the diversity were the
people living in the territory taken from Mexico. More recent refugees and
other immigrants from the Americas, Africa, Asia, and Europe add to the ever-
changing multicultural mosaic.

Colonists from western Europe chose to dominate rather than collaborate
with other populations (Takaki, 1993, 1994; Zinn, 2003); following conquests
of the indigenous peoples, English was established as the primary language.
Patterns of social, cultural, political, and economic oppression benefiting and
protected by descendants of western European immigrants emerged. Some
groups were privileged, while others were denied access to resources and
were silenced.

To consider history from diverse perspectives, ponder these scenarios,
imagining yourself as the actor in each one:

1. I am a middle-class African American woman from Georgia in my mid-thirties.
2. I am a white man who served in World War II. I am eighty-six years old. My pension fund is now in bankruptcy and Medicare Part D has changed. I can no longer afford my prescriptions.
3. I am a Cherokee woman. I am a lesbian. I live in the city but have strong ties to my home reservation.
4. I am an Asian American gay man. My great-grandfather came to the United States from Japan in the early twentieth century. My grandparents lived in California and were interned during World War II. My parents were born in the camps. I have good benefits at work but I cannot access benefits for my partner and our children.
5. I am a young white woman from Appalachia. My father and grandfather worked in the mines. The mines are closed and most of the families in our community are poor. I am the first person in my family to finish high school. I want to go to the local community college, but my parents don't understand and I am afraid the other students will laugh at the way I talk.

Ask yourself for each scenario whose lens you would use to view the history of the United States. How might you frame that history? How might that history affect the speaker's options and opportunities? Were the stories of the speakers reflected in the history you were taught as a child?

The History of Rights and Policies in the United States

Historically in the United States, people have been conferred rights and privileges based on race/ethnicity, gender and sex, sexual orientation, income, and class. Privilege and access to rights have been tied to whiteness, the concept of which has been constructed and defined by case law (Lopez, 1996). Specific rights were legally granted to those who were deemed "white" and were withheld from others. Whiteness was not simply the product of European heritage or a fair complexion. For example, throughout most of the 1800s, Irish immigrants were considered to be non-white and were relegated to housing and jobs alongside free blacks. The Irish finally established themselves as white by separating themselves from blacks by participating in their oppression (Ignatiev, 1995).

Public policies were tools used to limit the rights of women and people of color. Women did not receive the vote until 1920 (see Zinn, 2003, for a thorough history). Despite the fact that men of African descent received the right to vote when the Fifteenth Amendment to the Constitution was ratified in 1870, it was only after the Voting Rights Act of 1965, and subsequent related Supreme Court rulings between 1965 and 1969, that many African Americans were able to exercise their Fifteenth Amendment rights. It was not until 1924 that all Native

Americans were granted U.S. citizenship. While the framers of the U.S. Constitution were white male landholders who limited access to rights to white male landholders, the Constitution itself was framed liberally. Therefore, although amendments have expanded the group of people who are granted rights and privileges to include women and people of color, the legal system has been used to curtail the rights and freedom of various groups throughout the country's history. For example, *Plessy v. Ferguson* established de jure segregation with the separate but equal doctrine in 1896. This ruling was not overturned until *Brown v. the Board of Education* in 1954. Even then, one county in Virginia closed its public school system rather than allow racial integration. The country is still suffering the negative consequences of legalized segregation. The racism experienced by Chinese and Japanese immigrants and Chinese and Japanese Americans can be followed in case law as well. The Chinese Exclusion Act of 1882, the first law establishing an immigration quota based on race, excluded Chinese individuals from immigrating to the United States for ten years. The act was not repealed until 1943 when the United States agreed to allow 105 people of Chinese descent to immigrate each year, regardless of their country of origin. Executive Order 9066 authorized the internment camps for citizens of Japanese heritage during World War II. And in 1967, *Loving v. Virginia* established that states could not deny an individual the right to marry a person of a different race. It was not until 2000, however, that the last state law (in Alabama) banning interracial marriage was overturned. Case law regarding civil marriage between lesbian, gay, and transgender individuals is now being established in the United States, as well as globally. As the legal rights of lesbians and gay men are changing so quickly, you are encouraged to determine the current status of these laws.

Income and class are also significant variables that cross the lines of gender, race, and ethnicity. Economic inequality ebbs and flows, with noted periods of increased inequality, such as the industrial revolution of the late 1800s and the last several decades. Through institutionalized mechanisms, poverty is linked with race and gender (Collins & Veskel, 2004; Rothenberg, 2004). And income, while not synonymous with the socially constructed phenomenon of class, overlaps with social class (Liu, Soleck, Hopps, Dunston, & Pickett, 2004; Richardson, 2005; Wallerstein, 2000). The accumulation of wealth is the basis for people's access to resources, which means poverty has an intergenerational impact (Collins & Veskel, 2004). The accumulation of wealth in the United States was exacted through land acquisition and the systematic subjugation of people of color and other marginalized groups. The products of their labor, through enslavement and exploitation, belonged to factory and slave owners.

The federal Equal Employment Opportunity laws address and correct situations in which citizens are denied their rights. There are six federal laws prohibiting job discrimination based on gender, race, and disability: title VII of the Civil Rights Act of 1964, the Equal Pay Act of 1963, the Age Discrimination in Employment Act of 1967, titles I and V of the Americans with Disabilities Act of

1990, sections 501 and 505 of the Rehabilitation Act of 1973, and the Civil Rights Act of 1991. The U.S. Equal Employment Opportunity Commission enforces these laws through affirmative action plans and policies. As of January 2008, there are no federal laws protecting lesbian, gay, and transgender individuals (however, you are encouraged to examine current resources for possible changes in federal law).

Politics and the Economy

Unfortunately, people are not by nature accommodating beings (Freire, 1997). Rosaldo (1989) writes that "Questions of culture seem to touch a nerve because they quickly become anguished questions of identity" (p. ix). Change is frightening and occurs in spurts that are punctuated by reactionary backlashes. The widespread view that "things are the way they are because they cannot be otherwise" serves the purpose of maintaining the position of the economically and politically powerful (Freire, 1997, p. 36). As a result, a culture of silence continues to surround the institutionalized processes that create and maintain systemic oppression and privilege.

The political economy of capitalism practiced in the United States requires systems of oppression and inequality; these systems facilitate the exploitation of the many, which allows wealth to be concentrated in the hands of the few. After World War II, all groups experienced economic growth. That trend, however, has reversed in the last twenty years (Collins & Veskel, 2004). The rift between those who have wealth and those who don't has grown dramatically; during that time, households in the top 1 percent experienced the most growth. The top 1 percent "now has more wealth than the entire bottom 95 percent" (Collins & Veskel, 2004, p. 137). Poverty has increased as generations of youths grow up in an atmosphere of public greed (Ewalt, 1994; Pear, 2004). White men still have more wealth and higher incomes than women and people of color (Collins & Veskel, 2004; Rothenberg, 2004). This disparity in wealth is consistent across race: those at the top of each racial group have seen greater gains, and those at the bottom have actually experienced a drop in income (Collins & Veskel, 2004). Women make less than men, white men make more than men of color, and women of color have the lowest income (Rothenberg, 2004).

Single mothers who belong to lower socioeconomic groups are an example of a group that has been marginalized, stigmatized, and disempowered through economic, social, and political structures. Because women have less wealth and lower incomes than men, female-headed households suffer economically (Rothenberg, 2004). Limited work opportunities, legal constraints, the social and value judgments applied to mothers and mothering, and the historical threat of violence keep women confined and controlled. Single mothers, whose opportunities for higher education are limited, are relegated to nonprofessional wage labor jobs in which one's labor becomes the property of another. The message this sends regarding our commitment to the children whose life chances are inextricably tied to their adult caretakers' well-being is doubly troubling. The poverty too often experienced by female-headed single-parent families is the greatest risk factor faced by these families (Schmitz, 1995; Schmitz & Tebb, 1999).

Oppression keeps some groups marginalized by providing a ready labor pool of people willing to work for very low wages. Friedman (2006) challenges us to implement a flatter system with fewer low-skilled laborers, which would result in better relative pay. Wal-Mart, the nation's largest retailer and private employer, is an example of an organization that is both progressive and oppressive. They have developed cutting-edge global supply and delivery systems. At the same time, however, they do not provide adequate benefits for their employees and have employment practices that are being challenged in the courts (see box 1.2). The Denny's Corporation, on the other hand, provides an exemplar for change. Racial discrimination lawsuits in the 1990s tarnished Denny's reputation. Denny's responded with an action plan involving change at multiple levels. One of the first steps was to hire a diversity officer, who gradually changed discriminatory policies and corporate and employee behavior with the support of the CEO and the board of directors.

Box 1.2   Wal-Mart

For years, Activists Against Wal-Mart have accused Wal-Mart, the nation's largest retailer and private employer, of firing whistle-blowers, discriminating against women and African Americans, exploiting children and undocumented workers, union-busting, offering inadequate or no benefits and low pay, violating global human rights, and polluting the environment. This list of complaints and concerns goes on and is perhaps unprecedented in U.S. history. In 2005, Activists Against Wal-Mart launched a PR campaign to force the company to change its way of doing business. In 2006, Wal-Mart began to attempt to clean up its image while defending itself against the largest sex discrimination lawsuit in U.S. history in addition to other lawsuits as well. One alleged that Wal-Mart employees were forced to work without compensation. Another lawsuit, which alleged that undocumented workers were locked in stores overnight to clean, was settled out of court. One would think that these lawsuits and other allegations would have an effect on the company's profits. However, every day Wal-Mart continues to attract new customers.

Gina McCaskill

In August 2005 Hurricane Katrina demonstrated how race and class can affect response systems during a major disaster and in the recovery process (see box 1.3). The public housing projects and poorest neighborhoods in New Orleans, which were built in the lowest-lying areas of the city, were already vulnerable to flooding. When the levees broke, it was the most marginalized people who were unable to leave the city. Most of the people stranded were poor, and many were also disabled and elderly and did not have the means to leave the city. Because the city did not use its public transportation system to evacuate these residents, thousands were left stranded without food and water as hundreds of dead bodies floated in the streets. Many displaced residents feel that rebuilding is only benefiting those with resources and established networks.

Box 1.3   Hurricane Katrina

Since Hurricane Katrina ravaged the Gulf Coast states in August 2005, the city of New Orleans has undergone major changes. The cleanup process has been slow, the suicide rate has tripled (Saulny, 2006), and many residents have remained displaced. It has been reported that the black residents, who constituted 36 percent of the city's population before the storm, now make up only 21 percent of the population (Lyman, 2006). It appears that New Orleans and areas surrounding the city have grown increasingly white and middle class. Many African American and African and African Caribbean people were displaced, along with other families experiencing poverty. They have relocated throughout the United States.

It was the poorest residents who were left in the city and it is the poorest residents who have suffered the most in the recovery. The systems responding to Hurricane Katrina have been accused of disproportionately displacing many African Americans and families struggling with poverty, largely single women with children. The elderly and disabled have been equally affected by Hurricane Katrina. Residents of public housing in St. Bernard Parish returned home to be denied access to their apartments, and relatively few new public housing units have been opened. Public housing residents have accused the government of deliberately failing to supply adequate subsidized housing after the storm in order to encourage the poor to leave so that the area could be redeveloped. Many of the evacuees who were displaced will never have the resources they need to return home (see Pyles, 2006; Woods & Lewis, 2005).

On July 5, 2006, Mayor Nagin and other city officials unveiled a plan to rebuild the city. What remains uncertain is how working-class African Americans and other people in poverty from the Ninth Ward and other working-class areas will fare after the rebuilding. Will the city have an adequate amount of affordable and subsidized housing? Will there be reform in the public school system, which has historically failed to provide sufficient education to generations of the city's African Americans and others living in poverty? Will the health care system of a city that had one of the highest uninsurance rates in the United States before Katrina be rebuilt and be able to provide broader coverage (Rudowitz, Rowland, & Shartzer, 2006)? Will the record-breaking crime rates decline? Will the people living in poverty, who were disenfranchised prior to Katrina, have a voice in the rebuilding of the city? Will New Orleans residents who were displaced by the storm return to start their lives anew? Will the city make plans for evacuating the city's most vulnerable residents if the levees fail again? Most importantly, is there a place in the future New Orleans for the poorest of citizens?

Gina McCaskill

Those who amass excess wealth build political capital. Marginalized people, those who have been historically oppressed, are structurally disempowered through the denial of the resources they need to survive. The political capital of the wealthy has been used to influence the political process and the making of laws (Collins & Veskel, 2004). For transformation to occur, historically oppressed people must be involved in a decolonization process designed to grant them basic rights that should be afforded to all (see hooks, 1994, for related discussion). This transformation is an interactive process that requires the engagement of those with privilege in the growth and change process (Curry-Stevens, 2005). As a significant force in the change process, those who are historically oppressed have the ability to envision, create, and take action to attain justice (Freire, 1997). They must, however, work to develop the knowledge and heart to liberate themselves without becoming the oppressors. This development of consciousness provides a foundation for envisioning transformative action.

Collective Action

Collective identity and action are necessary for the transformation needed to end oppression and inequality. Hope for the future exists in the transformative nature of people (Freire, 1997). Social movements facilitate social change as the shift in critical consciousness occurs (Gil, 1998). The 1960s witnessed a shift in society's view of oppression and the rise of new social movements, starting with the civil rights movements, which focused on the needs of African American individuals and communities. The women's and gay, lesbian, and transgender movements followed. Most recently people with disabilities and now a slowly growing immigrant rights movement have begun to organize. However, it is possible for the process of social change not to move beyond the formulation of ideas; in order for social change to occur, "shifts in consciousness [must] cause individuals and groups to evolve new patterns of actions and social relations" (Gil, 1998, p. 57). This evolution depends "on self-transformation by individuals and social groups as well as on institutional transformations carried out collectively by individuals, groups, and networks among them" (Gil, 1998, p. 57).

Unless meaningful connections are made across historically oppressed groups, and links forged with privileged groups, meaningful change cannot occur. Coalition and ally building form the structural base for change. Without the collective action of allies, oppressed people remain disempowered. This leaves groups with privilege vulnerable as well. The risk of division was recognized by Martin Niemoeller, who stated: "In Germany they came first for the Communists, and I didn't speak up because I wasn't a Communist. Then they came for the Jews, and I didn't speak up because I wasn't a Jew. Then they came for the trade unionists, and I didn't speak up because I wasn't a trade unionist. Then they came for the Catholics, and I didn't speak up because I was a Protestant. Then they came for me, and by that time no one was left to speak up" (qtd. in Bartlett, 1992, p. 684). We no longer live in a world where we can exist in separate spheres. As Audre Lorde (1983) has said, "There is no hierarchy of oppressions" (p. 3). Bernice Johnson Reagon (2000) goes further when she states, "We've pretty much come to the end of a time when you can have a space that is 'yours only'—just for the people you want to be there....To a large extent it's because we have just finished with that kind of isolating. There is no hiding place. There is nowhere you can go and only be with people who are like you. It's over. Give it up" (p. 1105).

Social Work

As a result of dramatic changes in the U.S. population and policy, social work professionals are confronting diversity more directly and frequently than ever (National Association of Social Workers, 2001). Social work has the potential to lead change (Giroux, 1997). Critical multiculturalism is a theoretical and ideological stance that is compatible with the practice and values of social work. It is a concept that embraces diversity and opposes oppression (Schmitz et al., 2001). As social workers, more often than not, we serve and work with those who experience life as the "other," or those groups and individuals who fall outside what is defined as the norm—those who are kept at the margins. Our work is incomplete if we fail to address the systemic inequality they face.

Throughout the history of the social work profession, internalized oppression has existed within our ranks in spite of social work's effort to embrace diversity. Too often, the voices that have advocated change have been silenced. The code of silence within our professional and educational organizations keeps us from exposing workplace harassment, stigmatization, and violence, which most often affect women, people of color, people of different sexual orientations and gender identities, and people who are disabled. Classrooms and organizational and community spaces can and should become what McLaren (1997) calls "spaces of hope" that support individual and societal transformation. These spaces of hope and the transformative feelings they engender are not only individual and psychological but also structural and political.

Chapter 2

Self-Awareness, Critical Reflectivity, and Identity

> The unfinished character of human beings and the transformational character of reality necessitate that education be an ongoing activity. . . . The pursuit of full humanity, however, cannot be carried out in isolation or individualism, but only in fellowship and solidarity; therefore it cannot unfold in the antagonistic relations between oppressors and oppressed. No one can be authentically human while he [or she] prevents others from being so.
>
> Paulo Freire, *Pedagogy of the Oppressed*

While change begins within oneself, it does not occur in isolation. It can only occur in relation to others. As Bambara (1981) asserts in *The Bridge Called My Back*, "We have got to know each other better and teach each other our ways, our views, if we're to remove the scales . . . and get the work done" (p. vii). The goal of self-reflection within a critical multicultural context involves the development of an awareness of one's own identity, identity development in multiple dimensions, and increased awareness of economic and social structures of oppression as a foundation for activism.

Reflection facilitates the exploration of one's values, attitudes, and personal history, which can encourage ownership of and deepen responsibility for learning. Examining one's own biases and prejudicial attitudes, particularly when one is learning about and working with different identity groups, facilitates a process of change (Kondrat, 1999). A critical multicultural perspective enables one to evaluate how one's own behavior, speech, attitudes, and ways of interacting may contribute to biases or discrimination against people from marginalized groups. The goal is to identify and correct behaviors and attitudes and to break the cycle of oppressive and biased behaviors.

It is possible to explore the meaning of one's identity, examine the ways in which identity formation takes place, and understand the ways in which these identities influence how the world is experienced. Self-awareness is a necessary beginning. Being consciously and continuously aware of ourselves alters our relationships and is crucial when we are interacting with people whose backgrounds and lived experiences are markedly different from our own.

Our understanding of the self is ill defined and culturally based. It is difficult to engage in objective reflection about oneself. The very concept of self-awareness is socially constructed (Kondrat, 1999), which brings the process of attempting to engage in self-awareness full circle and illustrates the difficulty of grasping the concept. Kondrat identifies three types of self-reflection:

reflective self-awareness, reflexive self-awareness, and critical reflectivity. Through reflective self-awareness one examines oneself in order to become aware of personal biases and the interactive process of identity construction. Reflexive self-awareness is a process through which one becomes aware of how meaning is created through one's interactions with others. Critical reflectivity allows one to acknowledge oneself as both affecting and being affected by society and requires analysis of social structures. Critical reflectivity allows one to move beyond reflective self-awareness and reflexive self-awareness to a deeper level of understanding of oneself and one's assumptions, and how these interact with social structures (Kondrat, 1999).

The exercise in self-awareness developed by Elaine Pinderhughes (1989) asks people to think about race by reflecting on their life experiences (see box 2.1). This exercise facilitates a growth in self-awareness. It can help people recognize behaviors and attitudes that contribute to any "isms" (e.g., racism, sexism, heterosexism). Unfortunately, it can be difficult to recognize one's own biases, though it may be easier to recognize biases in others. Failure to recognize personal biases or negative attitudes toward others results in resistance to owning the possibility that one may be racist, sexist, or heterosexist (Kondrat, 1999). When a person examines her or his personal attitudes and behaviors in isolation from the larger social, political, and economic context, the structural barriers that impede the access to resources are not acknowledged. Neither the distortions of history nor the social construction of meaning is evaluated. This leads to racist acts and other oppressive practices. Individuals can fail to assess their own racist or biased thoughts and behaviors, as well as those of the community. Or they might acknowledge that biases do exist but feel that there is nothing they can do to change these situations (Kondrat, 1999).

Box 2.1   Self-Awareness Exercise

This assignment has two parts. First, respond to the questions below. Then, choose a family member or another significant person in your life who is either a generation older or younger than you. It is important that you do the self-interview first so that your interviewee's responses do not influence your answers. If you wish to share your answers with the person you interview, do so after you've completed the interview to avoid influencing your interviewee.

1. What is your ethnic or racial background? What has it meant to belong to this group?
2. Where did you grow up and what other racial/ethnic groups resided there?
3. What was your first experience with feeling different?
4. Did your family see itself as similar to or different from other ethnic groups?
5. What are the values of your racial/ethnic group?
6. What is your earliest memory of race or color?

7. What emotion did you experience?
8. With whom did you discuss this experience?
9. What are your feelings about being white or a person of color?
10. For people who are white: How do you think people of color feel about their color identity?
11. For people of color: How do you think people who are white feel about their color identity?
12. How have you experienced a sense of power or lack of power in relation to your racial/ethnic identity, family, class identity, gender, sexual orientation, and professional identity?

After transcribing the interviews, write a reflection paper about the interviews. Consider the following questions: How might your personal values, history, and experiences influence the way in which you view others? What are some of the similarities and differences you encountered between your answers and your interviewee's answers? In what ways might your interviewee's views influence your thinking? Has this exercise raised questions for you concerning your readiness to work with people from different cultures?

Source: Adapted from Pinderhughes, E. (1989). *Understanding race, ethnicity, and power: The key to efficacy in clinical practice.* New York: Free Press.

An approach that encompasses both oneself and the sociopolitical context breaks this gridlock. Advocates of critical reflectivity start with the supposition that all people and institutions somehow contribute to the oppressive behaviors and practices that perpetuate inequality (Kondrat, 1999). This suggests that one's daily interactions with others, whether conscious or unconscious, intentional or not, have broad and profound ramifications regarding racism, sexism, heterosexism, and ableism. Because one cannot wholly escape societal influences, one's conscious anti-racist convictions, attitudes, and behaviors do not exclude one from participation in the perpetuation of inequality. Racist and other oppressive acts are often perceived as overt actions, but inaction can produce the same results. What we do not know or are not conscious of can have unintended negative consequences for marginalized people.

When we consider the possibility that there may be alternative interpretations of reality, we allow ourselves to explore the significance and impact of our interactions with others. Assessing how we perceive and interact with people who are different from ourselves is a meaningful way to identify unconscious biases. The following questions reflect the spirit of critical reflectivity.

1. What do I do on a day-to-day basis that might contribute to inequality?
2. What have I learned about how to perceive or how to relate to members of my own group or other groups, and what is the source of that learning?

3. What do I know about how to relate to and interpret the behavior of others who occupy social locations (i.e., class, gender, race/ethnicity, sexual orientation, ability, religion) that are similar to, as well as different from, my own?
4. What have I learned about how to interpret the behavior of people whose race/ethnicity, sexual orientation, ability, or religion is different from my own? What if I add class and gender/sex to the equation?
5. What do I know about my conscious intentions when I interact with a client who is African American, Latino/Latina, Native American, Asian American, biracial or multiracial, or European American; refugees and other immigrants; people who are gay, lesbian, bisexual, transgender, or intersex; and people with disabilities?
6. Why do the consequences or outcomes of my actions not fit with or match my good intentions? (Kondrat, 1999)

These questions facilitate a process of reflection that allows for critical self-reflectivity. Box 2.2 provides an example of a situation in which this reflection was useful to a social work intern in her work.

Box 2.2   *Reflections of a Social Work Intern*

Carrie, a white social work intern in her mid-twenties, is completing her practicum in a community-based social service agency. She has been assigned several cases throughout the academic year. As she approaches her final two months of field work, she is asked to reflect on her experiences in preparation for the end-of-term field evaluation. Carrie was eager to start her internship and chose to work in an urban agency that had a diverse client population. Having been raised in a family that believed that all people should be treated equally, and having lived most of her life in a small rural all-white community, Carrie was looking forward to the challenges of an urban experience.

Carrie's agency is located in an active urban community that is home to a growing number of racial/ethnic groups. At this community service organization, clients can find a diverse range of services all under one roof. The rapid growth of the community, however, has required changes within the agency, which is now often short staffed. Although clients from various racial/ethnic groups are served, the agency staff is primarily composed of white middle-class women. Carrie looks to her colleagues and supervisor to understand agency protocol in this rapidly changing environment.

Carrie has demonstrated her willingness to actively engage in reflective practice through the use of supervision, journal writing, and field seminar discussions. Her weekly meetings with her supervisor have been very task focused, and she has received positive feedback about her performance. While reviewing her cases thus far, however,

Carrie and her supervisor noticed a pattern in some of her closed cases. Clients of other racial and/or ethnic groups have had less favorable outcomes than white clients. Carrie was concerned with this revelation. She is committed to the field of social work and believes in treating all people equally.

Carrie reviewed her cases and asked herself Kondrat's questions. As she evaluated her daily behavior, how she related to and interpreted the behavior of others, her intentions, and the consequences of her actions, she came to realize that in spite of her commitment to equal treatment, she inadvertently disregarded the history, culture, and value differences that significantly influence the way in which racial/ethnic identity affects an individual's experience of the world.

Reflection

Engaging in critical reflectivity offers an opportunity for the assessment of personal beliefs, intentions, and attitudes. The process highlights areas in which assumptions and interactions between oneself and others result in behaviors that perpetuate the marginalization of people who have been oppressed. This process reveals how power and privilege are understood or misunderstood, and how assumptions make a difference in determining whether interactions are productive, hurtful, or destructive. Categorical differences such as class, socioeconomic position, ability, sexual orientation, gender, and sex influence the interactions between members of privileged groups and people who are from historically oppressed populations. Critical reflectivity allows people to begin to understand how their experience of themselves is embedded in their interactions with others and how shared meanings are created (Kondrat, 1999). The focus is on examining the ways things can be changed, not on what could or should have happened. Moving beyond guilt, shame, or anger to critical reflection facilitates growth and the development of a new social consciousness (Schmitz et al., 2001). Misinformation that was received in the past can be corrected, and behavior modified in the future.

Understanding oneself in context allows one to search for new explanations for one's behavior and intentions (Schmitz et al., 2001). In this process, personal biases and cultural stereotypes, societal prejudices and oppression, and the experiences of all racial/ethnic groups in modern society are examined. It is within the context of our own experiences, relationships, family, community, and culture that we interpret our daily interactions. Understanding ourselves involves examining the norms, values, and skills arising from our own racial/ethnic, gender, socioeconomic, ability, and sexual orientation history and identification.

As we engage in the process, we come to recognize the disparities in power and authority between ourselves and others, and we begin to understand that our actions may have unintended consequences for others (Kondrat, 1999). Individuals who are white may recognize that they are members of a group that has historically oppressed people from other racial/ethnic groups, and that they are perceived as such by others. Collective knowledge of race relations and personal experience with racism may make people of color reticent to accept the actions of white individuals and groups. Similarly, white individuals and groups may feel the guilt and shame of racism, which can interfere with their interactions with others. Likewise, interactions between members of different populations of color are also influenced by assumptions, biases, and prejudices. Through dialogue it is possible to build bridges across difference.

One of the hidden phenomena of membership in a privileged group is the assumption of normality, according to which others are not normal. Assumptions are too often built on mythology and assumptions of one's own normality. For instance, the assumption that growing up in a multiracial family or a family with lesbian or gay parents can harm children is not based on data. People's interactions with others are influenced by myths like these. The consequences are destructive in social workers' work with children and families. With guidance, the experience of difference can lead to the development not only of a strong sense of self but also empathy, compassion, and understanding. Unexamined belief systems and ways of knowing are not adequate preparation for engaging in relationships in a multicultural environment. Racism, heterosexism and homophobia, sexism, transphobia, and ableism are pervasive in our society; even a person who sees her- or himself as unprejudiced can be guilty of these prejudices (Tatum, 1994). This realization can cause a broad range of emotions—including frustration, upset, shame, fault, and guilt (Schmitz et al., 2001). These uncomfortable feelings can create barriers to learning. Learning to recognize privileges that result from oppressive systems creates opportunities for creating change.

Examination of the learning process illuminates ways in which belief systems are shaped (see figure 2.1). We enter this world lacking assumptions. Through socialization by family, friends, and other people we respect and trust, we learn stereotypes, misinformation, myths, and partial histories that glorify some, vilify others, and erase people and events by making no mention of them at all. Misinformation acquired through early learning is reinforced by institutional and cultural structures such as the media, schools, religion, and governmental and legal systems, as well as traditions and customs. At each stage of learning we consciously, or unconsciously, accept what we have been taught. These truths, as we come to know them, shape how we see ourselves and how we view others. Our self-identity can be bolstered or deflated depending on the social strata we occupy. The sense of ourselves as racist, sexist, homophobic beings brings up a variety of emotions ranging from a false sense of superiority to a false sense of inferiority. Once new learning is internalized, the potential for making informed choices exists. We can decide to pass on the misinformation and act in ways that continue to marginalize people, or we can break the cycle and become allies with marginalized groups by acting responsibly.

FIGURE 2.1   Learning and Unlearning Assumptions of Hierarchical Social Orders

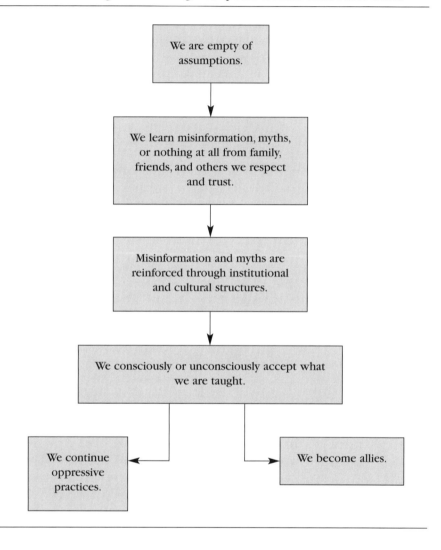

Identity Development

Identity development models are one tool for exploring similarities and differences between people of different racial/ethnic backgrounds, gender and sexual orientation, and ability status. There are also models that explore the development of people's identities in terms of gender, sex, sexual orientation, and ability status.

Race per se does not determine the quality of interactions between member of different racial groups. Racial identity development is a more salient factor (Carter, 1993). Racial identity development is not just something people who are white need to understand; populations that have historically been oppressed and marginalized because of their race must understand the process as well. Helms's (1993a) study of racial dyads highlights important implications for all people's understanding of racial identity development. Cognitive, affective, and behavioral issues are likely to influence different mechanisms that people use for coping with racial issues. The overlap between models of African American identity development and the model of white racial identity development further elucidates issues of identity, race, and racism. Tatum (2003) points out that all groups of color in the United States face issues regarding racism and as a result grapple with many of the identity development issues discussed by Helms (1993c), such as balancing the issues of assimilation into the dominate culture with the need to retain identification with one's own culture and community.

Racial identity development is neither static nor linear. Not everyone starts at the same place, nor does everyone progress in a step-by-step manner. The manner in which one's racial identity is integrated into her or his personality depends on several sociocultural factors, such as parents, family, peers, schools, religious organizations, and the media; systemic factors, such as socioeconomic class, discrimination, and quality of interracial interactions; and physical and personal attributes (Helms, 1993a).

African American Racial Identity Model

Theories of visible racial/ethnic identity in populations of color have been a topic of interest for several decades. William E. Cross and Janet Helms are among the leaders in this field of study. The model of racial identity development for people who are African American was first introduced by Cross (1978, 1980, 1991) and was later expanded by Helms (1984, 1993c, 1994). This model outlines the path that people who are African American may take in developing a healthy racial identity. Helms's (1993c) amended model, which focuses on one's worldview, delineates the five stages of racial identity formation: pre-encounter, encounter, immersion/emersion, internalization, and internalization/commitment.

During the pre-encounter stage, people who are African American idealize the worldview of the dominant white culture and denigrate blackness and black culture. It is assumed that people who are white hold their advantaged status because of their extraordinary efforts, and that people who are African American are disadvantaged because they have not exercised enough effort. The person denies her or his racial identity and identifies with people who are white. During this stage the person attributes her or his success or failure to how well she or he imitates the traits associated with whiteness (Helms, 1993b).

During the encounter stage, the person becomes aware that race is the delineator that determines or influences one's life options. A single event or an accumulation of events may lead to the realization that the Eurocentric world-view is no longer viable, and that another identity must be found. During the struggle to realize a new identity, she or he vacillates between shedding the pre-encounter identity and assuming a not yet clearly articulated African American identity. This phase is wrought with mixed emotions, ranging from confusion in the earlier stages to euphoria experienced at a later stage.

The immersion/emersion stage consists of two parts. First is the acceptance of a positive authentic African American identity and a black or Afrocentric worldview. The individual adopts an African American identity and abandons her or his previously constructed personal identity. The person might also overtly express a blackness that conforms to white stereotypes of blackness. During this stage African Americans may express anger toward people who are white, because they see them as the oppressors, and toward other African Americans who don't share their new perception of themselves. The individual experiences emotional ups and downs in trying to come to terms with a new identity and worldview. Immersion is a process of self-exploration, while emersion is a process of joining the community of identity to expand one's development. Emersion offers the possibility of escape from immersion. During emersion the person withdraws into a supportive African American community and engages in cathartic experiences. During this stage a person may engage in a range of social or political activities that allows exploration of African American and African cultural issues. The emersion into African American culture allows the person to develop a nonstereotypical Afro-American worldview.

The internalization stage marks the point at which one is able to positively internalize the unique elements of her or his personal identity blended with her or his African American identity. The person can now face the world from a position of strength and identifies with the African American group. The person rejects racism and other forms of oppression but can have positive relationships with supportive people who are white. Finally, internalization/commitment describes the continuation and nurturing of one's positive African American identity and involvement in social and civic activities that combat all forms of racism and oppression.

White Racial Identity Development

Far and away the most troublesome consequence of race obliviousness for many people is the failure to recognize the privileges our society confers on them because they have white skin. The privilege of white skin is a birthright, a set of advantages one receives simply by being born with features that society values (Dalton, 2002).

White people who fail to see themselves as racialized (that is, they tend not to think of themselves in racial terms) also fail to see the ways in which they are privileged. Peggy McIntosh (1990) wrote a landmark article about her own examination of her white privilege, in which she identified the many ways in which white people experience privilege. People who are white know that they are white, but this is often translated as being just American. They do not have any experience understanding race and how it shapes our lives. They typically don't think about their whiteness, nor do they think about the privilege bestowed on them because of their race.

This inability or unwillingness to think of oneself in racial terms has decidedly negative consequences. For one thing, it produces huge blind spots. It leaves people who are white baffled by the amount of energy many African Americans and other people of color pour into questions of racial identity. It makes it difficult for white people to understand why many people of color have a sense of group consciousness that influences the choices they make as individuals. It blinds them to the fact that their lives are shaped by race just as much as the lives of people of color. How white people view life's possibilities, whom they regard as heroes, the extent to which they feel the country is theirs, and the extent to which that belief is reinforced by society—all of this, and more, is a function of race. The internalized assumption of normality prevents them from imagining other possibilities.

Skin color is a complex social indicator that promotes differential power and privilege between people who are seen as white and people of color (Pinderhughes, 1989). One's perception of reality is seldom questioned, except when one stumbles upon others who are different and have opposing worldviews. This conflict offers people who are white the opportunity to develop knowledge and awareness of themselves as racial beings. People who are white are generally unaware of ways to develop a racial identity and have few opportunities to understand what it means to be white until they choose to embrace nonracist perspectives (Carter, 1995). White racial identity theory explains the developmental process that people who are white need to engage in to gain a better understanding of themselves and the environments in which they live. Exercises such as McIntosh's (1990) "White Privilege: Unpacking the Invisible Knapsack," a list of advantages that people with white skin experience in their daily lives and take for granted, can help individuals identify the ways in which they experience white privilege. These benefits range from being confident that one will not be discriminated against because of skin color in a job interview or when one tries to rent an apartment to seeing people of one's own race represented on television. This exercise (which is available online) can advance racial identity awareness, but her work also has implications for understanding how various marginalized groups are disadvantaged. If one substitutes "people of my own sexual orientation" or "others with a disability" for "people of my race" and "people of my racial group" in most of the situations described by McIntosh (for example, "I can, if I wish, arrange to be in the company of people of my race most of the time" or "I am never asked to speak for all the people of my racial group"), then one can see how unearned privilege benefits those who are heterosexual or able-bodied and disadvantages people who are gay, lesbian, bisexual, or people who have a disability.

Helms's (1993d) white racial identity development theory, called the abandonment of racism, runs parallel to the black racial identity development model and consists of six stages that occur in two phases (see figure 2.2). The process begins with the abandonment-of-racism phase, which has three stages: contact, disintegration, and reintegration. This is followed by the defining-a-nonracist-white-identity phase, which also involves three stages: pseudo-independence, immersion/emersion, and autonomy.

In the contact stage, people who are white develop a vague awareness of the presence of people of color. During this stage, people who are white may approach people of color with a tentative curiosity and may have only a vague or superficial awareness of their own whiteness. At this stage they still use their own whiteness as the norm against which they compare people of color, unaware that there are multiple ways to evaluate others. They pass judgment without understanding that whiteness is the norm against which they evaluate all others in terms of physical appearance, customs, values, behavior, and the like. Their interactions with people of color in social and occupational settings are limited, which means they have little opportunity to test their assumptions about people of color.

During the disintegration stage, whites start to develop a consciousness of whiteness. They begin what is sometimes a painful process of questioning what they have been taught and what they believe to be true. It is at this point that people who are white recognize that there are inequalities based on race and that social structures perpetuate oppression. They realize as well that their assumptions about whiteness and people of color are incorrect. Accepting that one is misinformed may also cause one to call into question one's ability to interact with people of color.

FIGURE 2.2   Stages and Phases of White Racial Identity Development

Phase 1 Abandonment of Racism

Phase 2 Defining a Nonracist White Identity

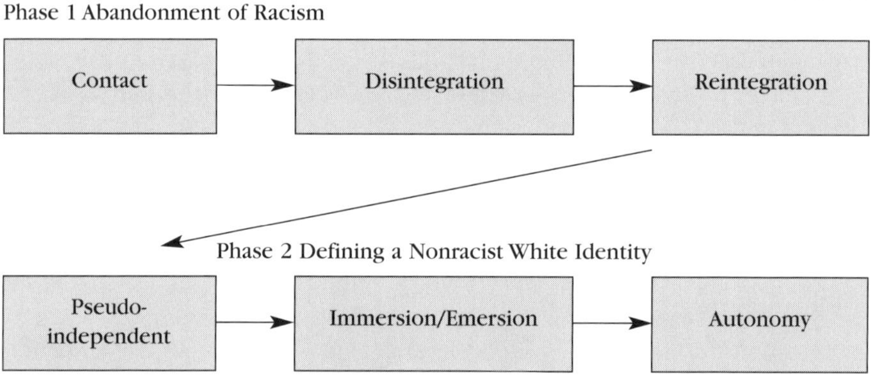

Source: Helms, J. (1993c). Toward a model of white racial identity development. In J. Helms (Ed.), *Black and white racial identity*. Copyright © 1993 by Janet E. Helms. Reproduced with permission of Greenwood Publishing Group, Inc., Westport, CT.

During reintegration, the third stage of phase 1, people have acknowledged their white identity but assume that the social structures that privilege them and disadvantage others are part of a natural order. During this stage, people selectively process or reinterpret the world around them to align with the social mores that encourage stereotypes of people. They often minimize or deny similarities that they observe between people who are white and people of color.

During pseudo-independence, the first stage of the second phase, the individual begins the formation of a positive white identity, engaging in an intellectual process in an effort to make sense of what she or he has learned. Assumptions, including notions of superiority and inferiority based on race, are questioned in earnest. The person begins to acknowledge that she or he has a responsibility to help dismantle the system of oppression of people of color. Yet people at this stage may still behave in ways that inadvertently maintain the status quo. They may now see people of color as victims but may also believe that the solution to the problem is to help people of color adopt the culture of the white dominant society. They do not yet see racial differences as viable alternative ways of being. They still measure all people against the white ideal. During this stage, the motives of individuals who are earnest about developing a positive white racial identity may be questioned by the racial groups they are trying to champion and may be viewed with suspicion by family members or other people they know who are white. Those who are encouraged to continue the campaign against race-based social injustice are well on their way to developing a racial identity that no longer privileges whiteness and marginalizes people of color.

Immersion/emersion is the period during which people develop a strong commitment to the development of a positive white racial identity, and to replacing myths and stereotypes about whiteness and people of color with accurate information. The questions that are asked at this stage are "Who am I racially?" "Who do I want to be?" and "Who are you really?" People often facilitate this journey by reading about others who are white who have engaged in racial identity struggles or by participating in white consciousness-raising groups that are committed to addressing racial injustice. At this stage, individuals no longer see people of color as needing to be fixed. They fully accept the need for people who are white to play an integral role in the change process.

Autonomy, the final stage, describes the internalization of a new definition of whiteness and a commitment to nurture this identity. The person is now committed to eliminating oppressive behaviors; she or he no longer vilifies or pays tribute to others based on their group membership. While developing an autonomous racial identity, the person also seeks out opportunities to engage with members of other racial and cultural groups. This final stage of white racial identity does not represent the end of racial identity development, but a new beginning that must be nurtured, encouraged, and respected. This stage marks the individual's acceptance that this is an ongoing process requiring openness to new information and different worldviews. Tatum (1994) describes the final stage as much like a spiral staircase that allows the individual to revisit previous stages before moving forward. As in the final stage in African American identity development, the person no longer feels the need to pass judgment on others based on group membership.

Alternative Models of Identity Development

Helms's models of racial identity development for African Americans and whites are conceptualized in stages that focus on actions rather than outcomes. The stages describe a series of experiences that force us to ask who we are and to question our identity. Since the appearance of racial identity development models in the literature, the concepts described in these models have been used to describe the experiences of other cultural groups, which suggests comparable processes and experiences among marginalized groups (Sue, Carter, Casas, Fouas, Ivey, Jensen, et al., 1998). The experiences of people who are from non-Western cultures may be different and the process of identity development that they go through may be different as well, and some people have argued that Helms's model does not represent their own experiences. Sue and Sue (1993), for instance, present a model of identity development for Asian Americans that focuses on historical, familial, and cultural issues. This does not mean that Helms's model should be discarded. In fact, Tatum (2003), in support of the Helms model, identifies some issues regarding identity development in racist environments that affect all communities of color. Stage models and other models for understanding different ways of being and knowing can be used in parallel with each other, as each is a legitimate way of explaining the identity development process. Examining other models minimizes hierarchal ordering and allows one to embrace and honor all ways of knowing.

Wilson (1996) believes that indigenous Americans' embrace of the interconnectedness between the person and her or his multiple environments is a useful alternative to the singularly focused racial/ethnic identity model proposed by Helms, which does not account for simultaneous experiences of difference. Intersecting and simultaneous oppressions must be assessed, as they change the context and content of an individual's experience and may also change how one's identity is understood.

The experiences of Native Americans are often conveyed through storytelling, a method that has not been commonly used in Western research. Storytelling and narratives, however, are an integral part of indigenous knowledge building and research. Stories can be powerful and can contribute to a collective story in which the experiences of every indigenous person can be heard (Smith, 1999). Horse (2001) uses story and history to present a model of identity development for Native Americans. He presents a model that crosses the individual and group, incorporating history, language and culture, traditions, and spirituality. In the end, personal and cultural identities remain intertwined.

Like Native Americans, Asian Americans may experience different identity development pathways. Few models of identity development have been constructed with an Asian identity development in mind (Yeh & Huang, 1996). Sodowsky, Kwan, and Pannu (1995) proposed a model of Asian ethnic identity that considers the complex interactions between the individual and the context in which she or he is placed. This model is nonlinear and bidirectional, which means that it views an individual's ethnic identity orientation as situational and changing over time (Chae, 2001/2002). The extent and degree of one's acculturation into the dominant cultural can have a direct influence on one's ethnic identity. The nonlinear ethnic identity process "does not arise out of labiality or stability, rather it arises out of the ethnic individual's adaptive principles of flexibility and openness to possibilities" (Sodowsky et al., 1995, p. 145).

Sue and Sue (1993) examine the impact of Asian cultural values and cultural and legal racism on the identity development of Asian Americans. In Asian cultures, loyalty to one's family and community has a higher value than autonomy and independence. Restraint of emotion is valued. These values conflict with many of the dominant culture values in the United States. Kim (2001) looks at how Asian Americans resolve these conflicts. She presents an Asian American identity development theory that consists of five stages: ethnic awareness, white identification, awakening to social political consciousness, redirection to an Asian American consciousness, and incorporation of a positive identity as Asian American. Similar to Helms's model of racial identity development for African Americans, Kim's theory involves a movement from idealization of whiteness to an increased appreciation of one's own culture and an increased social and political consciousness.

Models of identity development for Latinos and Latinas are complex since commonly used racial categories do not fit, as a person can be both Latino/ Latina and a member of any of the other racial groups (Ferdman & Gallegos, 2001). The complexity is intensified by the diversity of cultures and cultural identification. Ferdman and Gallegos (2001) identify five starting points for Latino/Latina identity development that are linked to self-identification as a Latino/Latina: Latin-integrated, Latino-identified, subgroup-identified, Latino as other, undifferentiated/denial, and white-identified. Torres and Baxter (2004) explore models of identity development for Latino and Latina college students with a focus on the impact of education on image development. They have found that exposure to a learning environment in which individuals can explore their ethnic/cultural environment and reconstruct their view of the world allows them to appreciate its complexity. This has a positive effect on identity development. Models of identity development for multiracial people are growing in complexity as people refuse to accept simplistic categorization. Kich (1992) and Poston (1990) have developed stage models of multiracial identity development; however, these models have been criticized as inadequate for encompassing the complexities of multiracial people (Wijeyesinghe, 2001). The factor model of multiracial identity considers eight factors that affect the choices of multiracial people: racial ancestry, cultural attachment, early experience and socialization, political awareness and orientation, spirituality, other social identities, social and historical context, and physical appearance (Wijeyesinghe, 2001).

Models exploring gender and sexual orientation identity development both overlap and differ. The development of gender roles and gender identity is commonly contested and open to debate. The role of biology in gender is only vaguely understood. Current research with transgender and intersex individuals both clarifies and clouds our knowledge of gender and gender identity. As we come to understand transgender identity, it has become obvious that linear models cannot explain all paths to identity development (Bilodeau & Renn, 2005). What is clear is that if there are biological components to the development of gender, they do little more than establish predispositions and tendencies. "Gender, like race, does become a social construction when it is treated as a categorical, fixed difference and then used to deny opportunity and equality to women" (Healey, 2003, p. 24). In exploring the relationship between feminist identity development and gender roles and well-being, Saunders and Kashubeck-West (2006) have found that feminist identity correlates positively with psychological well-being. Downing and Roush (1985) present a model of feminist identity development derived from Cross's model of racial identity development. Moradi (2005), who has examined the literature on womanist identity development, proposes the womanist identity development model as one that facilitates the simultaneous exploration of gender, race, and ethnicity. The little research that has been done shows correlations between feminist and racial identity development. Likewise, Hoffman (2006) found correlations between gender and ethnic identity and self-acceptance.

Many of the gender identity and sexual orientation developmental models are linear, though recent research incorporates knowledge development in the biological arena. Hunter (2005) thoroughly reviews the professional literature on the development of lesbian, gay, bisexual, and transgender identities. Most models of lesbian, gay, bisexual, and transgender identity are stage models that describe a linear progression across stages. The models are dated and simplistic in many respects (Hunter, 2005). While many look at these characteristics in isolation, some are more holistic, taking into consideration the impact of race and ethnicity on sexual orientation identity (Bilodeau & Renn, 2005). Parks, Hughes, and Matthews (2004), who explored racial and ethnic differences within sexual orientation, found support for a model of development in which timing and spacing of the phases are not rigid and fixed. They found that African American women and Latinas experienced similar processes, while white women were older when they first decided to explore their sexual orientation, faster in making decisions about their orientation, and quicker to disclose to others. White lesbians were more likely than lesbians of color, who must integrate their development as women of color with their sexual orientation development, to disclose their sexual orientation to people outside their families. Parks, Hughes, and Matthews hypothesize that their development as members of one historically oppressed group may help prepare lesbians of color for developing a healthy identity as members of a group that is oppressed because of sexual orientation; white women do not have that experience upon which to draw. Cramer and Gilson (1999) have found similarities between the identity development models for lesbian, gay, and bisexual individuals and for individuals with disabilities. They propose the use of a fluid model that recognizes the biopsychosocial-cultural context and the impact of language and multiple identities.

Finally, Chestang's (1972, 1984) theory on character development in a hostile environment focuses on the impact of social injustice and social inequality on personal and racial identity development. The struggle against abuse, forbearance, and the need to persevere affect the development of racial identity and group identification. According to Chestang's theory of the depreciated or transcendent character, the combined impact of social injustice and inconsistency results in a feeling of personal impotence and inadequacy. Although all individuals who have been oppressed have developed both a depreciated character and a transcendent character, one becomes dominant. The depreciated character generally accepts what is and does not seek change; she or he accepts and navigates the oppressive system. She or he assimilates. On the other hand, the transcendent character forces change, finding innovative ways to change society's inconsistencies while advocating social justice and empowerment. Hope and optimism become the driving force to develop an equitable system for all. Transcendent characters are change agents.

Models for understanding identity development are useful tools because they provide a framework and structure that can help us formulate questions about who we are in relation to our interactions with others. Using these frameworks as blueprints, however, can lead to stereotyping and essentializing. Using models as the sole mechanism for understanding complex behaviors can cause one to disregard the complex interactions that can take place between different characteristics such as race/ethnicity, sex and gender, and sexual orientation.

Multidimensional Identity Development

Models of identity development are often unidimensional and therefore fail to acknowledge the interactions that occur between race, ethnicity, gender identity, sexual orientation, and ability. Consequently, they often do not validate multiple layers of oppression (and privilege). Privilege may go unrecognized, regardless of its source, and those with privilege may continue to oppress others. For instance, heterosexuals and able-bodied people, regardless of class, race, and gender, may perpetrate or reinforce oppressive and biased acts against those who are lesbian, gay, bisexual, transgender, or intersex and people with disabilities. Each individual in a multicultural society must be attuned to her or his own attitudes, beliefs, and actions. Table 2.1 shows a stage model

TABLE 2.1   Stages of Identity Development

Stage	Perceptions of difference	Stages	Results of privilege
Pre-encounter	Unawareness of one's own whiteness, masculinity, heterosexuality, or able-bodiedness	Contact	Obliviousness to one's own racial identity, heterosexuality, able-bodiedness; differential privilege; and the existence of gender beyond the male-female dichotomy
Encounter	Consciousness of race, gender diversity, sexual orientation, and disability	Disintegration	First acknowledgment of white identity, gender diversity, heterosexual identity, and able-bodiedness
		Reintegration	Idealization of whites, males, heterosexuals, and able-bodied individuals; denigration of blacks, transsexual and intersexual individuals, gays, lesbians, bisexuals, and people with disabilities
Immersions/ Emersion	Idealization of own race, gender, sexual orientation, and ability status	Pseudo-independence	Intellectual acceptance of one's own and others' race from the white perspective, of gender and of sexual identity from the dominant perspective, and of disability from a perspective of able-bodiedness
Internalization	Transcendence of race, gender, sexual orientation, and ability status	Immersion/ Emersion	Honest appraisal of racism and the significance of whiteness in the maintenance of oppression; sexism in the maintenance of male privilege and the marginalization of transsexual and intersex people; heterosexism and the significance and the roles of heterosexism and homophobia in the oppression of lesbians, gays, and bisexuals; ableism and the significance of able-bodiedness
Commitment	Activist	Autonomy	Internalization of a multicultural non-racist non-sexist, non-heterosexist, and non-ableist identity; commitment to work toward the alleviation of racism, sexism, and toward other necessary changes

of identity development for members of marginalized groups. This stage model depicts the overlap between two models of identity development and attempts to move the application beyond race to other sources of identity. As people who are marginalized because of gender and sex, sexual orientation, or ability develop awareness of themselves and of others, they experience stages similar to those depicted in the model. As one moves from the pre-encounter stage to the encounter stage, awareness grows. Consciousness expands through self-reflection and involvement with one's communities of identity. Internalization and commitment follow. As we grow in the areas of life where we experience oppression, we must also grow in the areas where we experience privilege. This model can be adapted to types of privilege beyond those created by race, which helps individuals recognize the assumptions of normality that they have internalized.

Investigating one's self-identity and how it interferes with the ability to understand multiple worldviews creates opportunity for change. Start by examining your relationships and the patterns they follow. Who is in your family and your social and community circles? With whom do you socialize? What activities do you attend, and who else attends? How do you behave and interact with people from different cultures and communities? How can you create opportunities to form supportive and meaningful relationships with people from other cultures and communities? Becoming an agent for equality in a multicultural society requires one to accept this as a journey, not a destination. It also requires us to live with vulnerability as we navigate new paths and grow to understand, if not accept, other ways of knowing and being.

Chapter 3

Race and Ethnicity

Seeking no favors because of our color or patronage because of our needs, we
knock at the bar of justice and ask for an equal chance.

Mary Church Terrell, *What Role Is the Educated Negro Woman
to Play in the Uplifting of Her Race?*

Folktales and fairy-tales, the stories of our youth, often have difficulty making
the transition to adulthood. In recent years, the parables that convey messages
for life have been challenged. For example, we now try to teach girls that Prince
Charming isn't coming to the rescue. Can one really envision a relationship
book stressing the importance of kissing frogs in order to find a prince? The
ugly duckling, another fairy-tale, is perhaps one of the first literary characters
of color that those socialized into dominant U.S. society can remember. He is
marked from birth as different by appearance because he is larger and darker
than the others. As a result, he is not accepted by the white ducklings, who
taunt and ridicule him. In his sadness, he wanders off, hoping to find acceptance. The duckling grows up to change into a beautiful white swan and then
becomes the envy of all the swans on the lake. For a child of color, this fairy-
tale seems to suggest that one must change one's color or culture in order to
succeed. The story does not describe the experiences of people of color or
many ethnic groups whose needs cannot be addressed by superficial changes,
nor does it recognize that structural and institutional barriers prevent some of
our children from realizing the dream of full inclusion. The barriers are social
and economic, not individual.

The Social Construction of Race

Race is a social construction that is essentially the product of social thought
and relations. It is a concept that has different meaning to different people and
the term itself can be inflammatory. Scientists have established that race is not
linked to genetics. Although people from different continents may have different color skin, eye shape, height, and hair type, these physical characteristics
determine only a small part of who we are as humans (Delgado & Stefancic,
2001). The social sciences have come to reject biological notions of race and
now embrace the concept of race as a social construction.

Race consciousness and theories of race are a modern phenomenon (Omi
& Winnant, 1994), and critical multiculturalism asks how such boundaries are
used, and for whose benefit. Popular culture mediates images of what is be-

lieved to be the norm, which changes over time. These images often foster the belief that only certain groups, particularly white people, have contributed to the development of society. What is glaringly absent from the U.S. cultural scene is the recognition that each group in the United States makes rich and positive cultural contributions to society.

The concept of race is embedded in social and historical contexts. The meaning of race has varied throughout history and has been a matter of much debate. Social, economic, and political institutions have been instrumental in determining the content and importance of the racial categories society has created. Omi and Winnant (1994) have observed that "Once we understand that race overflows the boundaries of skin color, super exploitation, social stratification, discrimination and prejudice, cultural domination and cultural resistance, and state policy—once we recognize the racial dimension present to some degree in every identity, institution and social practice in the United States—once we have done this, it becomes possible to speak of racial formation. This recognition is hard-won; there is a continuous temptation to think of race as an essence, as something fixed, concrete and objective" (p. 17).

Over time, racial categories develop and fall out of usage in response to different social movements. The ways in which racial categories change demonstrate the uncertainty inherent in our constructions of race. "Racial categories are often used as ethnic intensifiers with the aim of justifying the exploitation, marginalization, and violence of one group by another" (Walker, 2003, p. 667). Notions of racial identity have been altered at different points in time, as is reflected in the revision of categories for capturing information on race and ethnicity in the 2000 U.S. census. By changing its practices, the federal government recognized the lack of clarity in the definition of racial identity. It also acknowledged the need to adjust racial definitions to reflect a changing social understanding of race as well as to respect the right to individual self-identification.

Although race scholars have understood for decades that race is a social construction, racial classification based on physical traits has become so engrained in the American psyche that getting people to think otherwise is a major challenge. The scientific validity of race is of little import. It is society's belief that race exists that provides its significance (Marger, 1997). The definition of race is so entrenched in everyday discourse that we note the differences between people based on physical features, including skin color. We wonder, if these are not people of different races, if there are differences and, if so, what they signify. The problem is with what is believed to be a commonsense understanding of race.

Scholars' growing understanding of race as a social construction does not mean that people of color do not continue to be marginalized based on socially constructed racial classifications. Within these centuries-old structures, which place power and privilege in the hands of the dominant group, legacies continue to affect the social standing of groups. As Daniel (2002) states, "Even people who maintain that race is an illusion recognize the social reality of race in the West and cannot avoid using the term even as they deny its existence" (p. xiii).

Racism

Racism is structured around three flawed basic assumptions. First is the assumption that people can be divided into discrete categories based on biological race. Second, these divisions are believed to be intrinsically connected to culture and individual characteristics such as personality and intelligence. Finally, it is assumed that due to biological race, some groups are naturally superior to others (Marger, 1997). The very ordinariness of racism is what makes it so difficult to change. It is the common way of doing business and benefits people who are white across classes (Delgado & Stefancic, 2001).

Perhaps because of affirmative action policies, many people today believe that racism no longer exists, and that class is what matters most. Yet many states have a human rights commission that hears cases and makes decisions on claims of racism regularly. People's first inclination is to see racism as tied to overtly racist regimes under which the unequal treatment of people based on race is bureaucratized and rationalized, such as apartheid in South Africa and our own history of slavery. But racism takes on many disguises. Racism has become institutionalized (i.e., normalized) to the point that we tolerate it as part of everyday life. Racism can be subtle or blatant, overt or covert. It can disguise itself in everyday interactions; it can rear its head in the unintended consequences of policy and practice.

Racism is not just a personal ideology but a system of cultural messages and institutional policies and practices, as well as individual beliefs and actions. In the United States, this system clearly operates to the advantage of whites and to the disadvantage of people of color. Racial prejudice, when combined with social power and access to social, cultural, and economic resources and decision making, leads to the institutionalization of racist policies and practices. Racism is a structural issue, and only those with the political and economic power to oppress others can be racist (Bivens, 1995). So, while people from any ethnoracial group can be prejudiced or biased or practice discrimination, only those with the resources to oppress other groups systemically and structurally can be racist.

The evaluation of advantage and disadvantage is critical to the examination of racism in the United States (Tatum, 2001). Some of the social and political manifestations of racism can be seen in past laws. These include the forbidding of interracial marriage and the implementation of separate facilities, including drinking fountains, schools, and bathrooms, for blacks and whites. Racism can be seen in policies and practices that structure barriers to keep people of color from gaining equal access to resources such as quality education, decent housing, and other economic opportunities that would enable them to rise up from poverty. The social and political manifestations of racism can also be seen in other countries. For example, in South Africa, under apartheid, access to goods and services for all non-white people was systematically controlled. The strictest limitations were applied to people with the darkest skin color (Patterson, 1953). Nazi Germany also engaged in mass genocide in an attempt to create a perfect society made up of a "perfect" white, blond, blue-eyed "race."

The Social Construction of Whiteness

Because people who are white do not generally perceive themselves in racial terms, discussions about race usually refer to African Americans, Latinos/Latinas, Asians, and Native Americans but rarely to whites. When forced to acknowledge their whiteness, they see it as not being black, or not being the "other." This allows them to avoid acknowledging the centrality of ethnoracial identity in both daily interactions and systemic economic and political structures.

Although the term "white" is as much a social construct as the term "race," the denial of its existence grants those with white skin a special status, which reinforces widespread misery. Whiteness is an unearned status in a society that claims to be a meritocracy, in which people advance based on talent, intellect, and achievement. In recent decades, scholars from many fields, including critical race theorists, have rejected the assumption that analyzing race means focusing primarily on people of color and have embraced the critical study of whiteness (e.g., Allen, 1994; Roediger, 1999; Omi & Winnant, 1994).

Although whiteness has become the norm, the standard for being, this was not always the case. It was not until the end of the seventeenth century that an interest in white identity developed. The institutionalization of the system of race privilege made it necessary to make clear distinctions between blacks and whites (Allen, 1994). A legal definition of whiteness was not established until immigration laws were drafted in 1790 and the courts began making decisions concerning who could and could not live in the United States and what rights those living in the United States would have. Judges defined whiteness based on prejudices of the time as the absence of blackness, an opposition that marked a boundary between those with privilege and those without. Only those deemed white were worthy of entry into the United States under early immigration statutes (Lopez, 1996).

The ever-changing construction of whiteness has allowed some groups to become part of the so-called white race. Early in U.S. history, Irish, Jews, and Italians were considered non-white and were regarded as lower forms of beings, as were African Americans and other recent immigrants. Over time, some of these immigrants gained entry into mainstream white culture by joining with the dominant group in maintaining structures of oppression and by acquiring wealth through legal and sometimes illegal means.

Since race is a social construction based on hierarchical divisions of power and privilege, the concept of whiteness has been invisible. Lopez (1996) calls this the "transparency phenomenon," whereby people's whiteness renders them invisible or transparent. As a result of this phenomenon, people who are white have the privilege of not being conscious of their own race and are not required to understand the implications of being white. The invisibility of whiteness allows many people who are white to believe they are normal, the standard by which all others are judged. Wildman and Davis (2002) write that "The invisibility of privilege strengthens and maintains the power it creates. The invisible cannot be combated, and as a result privilege is allowed to perpetuate, regenerate, and re-create itself. Privilege is systemic, not an occasional occurrence. Privilege is invisible only until looked for, but silence in the face of privilege sustains it invisibility" (p. 89).

Many scholars who have written about white privilege have examined their own privilege in doing so. For these scholars, the process of writing facilitated a journey of discovery about the many ways in which they have benefited from this unearned position. Their contributions to this subject have been important on many levels. These explorations are useful because it is often difficult for those who have experienced a lack of privilege and thus are familiar with the outsider position to understand how one group of people can be blind to systems of privilege that are transparent to those who are on the outside.

Ethnicity and Ethnoracial Identity

Ethnicity, like race, is socially constructed. Because the use of this word tends to vary widely and is imprecise and subjective, some social scientists prefer not to use it as a descriptor. Ethnicity is fluid, flexible, layered, and dependent on circumstances and context; ethnic identity is affected by cultural elements, affiliative dimensions (selection of friends and acquaintances from one's own ethnic group, as well as behavior and dress), and subjective dimensions (perceptions of those within and outside the ethnic group of which one is a member). The final element of ethnic identity is ethnic pride, which provides a sense of attachment to an ethnic group (Kulis, Napoli, & Marsiglia, 2002). The manner in which individuals embrace ethnic identity may or may not involve all four dimensions.

An ethnic group is composed of people who share a sense of attachment on the basis of cultural criteria and a shared history. It can be tempting to use ethnicity instead of race as an identifier because it appears to move away from the notion that this source of identity is biological or natural (Smedley, 2007). Unfortunately, the literature on ethnicity focuses much of its attention on white ethnic groups and dedicates too little attention to "visible ethnics" such as blacks (e.g., Africans, people from the Caribbean), Latinos/Latinas (e.g., Mexicans, people from Central and South America, Puerto Ricans, Cubans), Asians (e.g., Chinese, Japanese, Koreans, Vietnamese, Filipinos), and different Native American nations and tribes (Pierre, 1977).

Although race is a social construction that is arbitrary, not fixed, but dynamic and changing over time, the concept of race can serve as an indicator of institutional racism (Hollinger, 2003; Outlaw, 1996). Because we live in a society that is socially mobile and no longer has legal barriers to interracial marriages, it can be difficult to identify boundaries separating one racial group from another. In fact, these boundaries do not exist, and when we use the concept of race in this way, we run the risk of perpetuating the idea that race is a biological reality, not a social construct. What is important to understand is how populations self-identity across cultural, affiliative, and subjective dimensions. This is far more important than knowing where they fit within the socially constructed categories established by the federal census registry.

Current scholars of race and ethnic relations have adopted the concept of ethnoracial identity to more accurately describe the complexity of people's experiences and to acknowledge how the concepts of race and ethnicity have collided in U.S. history. The theoretical construct of ethnoracial identity forces us to remember that history, people's physical attributes, and culture define the course of people's lives. Ethnoracial identity acknowledges that people respond to both physical and cultural cues in others. Ethnoracial groups are neither simple nor static categories. They are social relationships through which people distinguish themselves from others (Fenton, 1999).

Research on the different groups that have become known collectively as Latinos and Latinas indicates that requiring people to claim an ethnic/racial identity based on one's place of origin is simplistic and inadequate. The latest federal census results puzzled researchers because more than 40 percent of all Latinos/Latinas choose "other" rather than the Hispanic/Latino category. Duany (2002) surmises that the popular use of the terms "Hispanic" and "Latino" and "Latina" has allowed many Puerto Ricans, for example, to avoid choosing between black and white and instead identify as Puerto Rican and Hispanic or Latino/Latina, thereby claiming for themselves a nationality and a race. The either-and approach has become popular among people of multiple other ancestries as well.

The categories of race and class can be limiting when they are used in practice, rather than theory, with people in need of services rather than as abstract concepts. Ethnoracial positioning can provide a more accurate understanding of an individual, family, or community. In exploring ethnoracial identity, one moves beyond categories such as black or white to look at the values, beliefs, attitudes, activities, behaviors, and practices that affect people's daily lives and community identification. For instance, if we categorize people by race and class, a black family living in a major city may be labeled poor and black. However, if we consider ethnoracial positioning, we might learn about the language spoken at home by this family, which could be Spanish, French, English, or one of the many African languages. We might learn about different aspects of their culture, such as child-rearing practices, milestone celebrations, kin relationships, and gender role expectations. Illness and health, as well as the role of authority, are viewed in different ways depending on the family's ethnoracial identification. Depending on their ethnoracial identification, the family could experience support or marginalization within the larger black community. All these factors related to ethnoracial identification allow for a deeper understanding than the concepts of race and class alone.

Mixed Race/Ethnicity

Hollinger (2003) has written a compelling historical overview of the ethnoracial mixture in the United States that helps us to understand the sociocultural structures that created race classifications and divisions. The United States has a rich ethnoracial heritage; its population consists of the descendants of individuals from more nations than any other industrialized country in the North Atlantic. Hollinger notes that statutes on marriage illustrate this situation. The prohibition of interracial marriages, or miscegenation, the goal of which was to prevent black-white unions, was a central theme of political discourse during the 1860s, the period during which slavery was legally abolished. The primary motivation for such statutes was to prevent the offspring of white men and black women (who were most often slaves) from inheriting property. The last vestiges of these laws were not abolished until the 1960s with *Loving v. Commonwealth of Virginia*. Miscegenation laws were not equally applied across all racial/ethnic groups; for example, only twelve states banned marriage between whites and Native Americans, and enforcement was often lax.

Blackness is often treated as a monolithic identity: an individual either is or is not black, based on the principle that any African ancestry makes a person black. During the Jim Crow era fractional classifications were created to separate people by degree of African blood. Privilege was determined by the quantity of black blood a person possessed. After the 1920 federal census, the term "mulatto" was dropped, which meant that whites were now viewed as people with no trace of black blood, and all others became non-white.

In 1923, Congress declared that people from South Asia were non-white, and some miscegenation statutes listed Oriental or Mongolian as racial categories, along with Negro. The miscegenation statutes regarding Asians were primarily enforced in the western states, where anti-Asian sentiment was high. This culminated with the internment of Japanese Americans on the West Coast during World War II. Finally, in the late 1940s, California deemed the miscegenation statutes unconstitutional. As anti-Asian prejudice declined, people of Asian descent became more incorporated into the social order.

Newcomer Latino/Latina populations create a dilemma for federal policies of the United States because, according to the classifications defined by the U.S. Census Bureau, one can be both Latino/Latina and a member of another racial group. The label of Latino/Latina challenges the system of classification because this category is less strictly color marked than a category such as black or white. Many immigrants from Mexico, for example, are descendents of whites and Native Americans. Latinos/Latinas were usually regarded as legally white even when they were stigmatized and mistreated. Marriages between Mexicans and

Asians were not usually contested, but marriage between Mexicans and blacks was seen as crossing the color line.

The federal government eventually recognized that some Latinos/Latinas were black and others were white. The Census Bureau adopted the term "Hispanic non-white" for the 1970 census. Ethnic/racial classifications for Latino/Latina recognize that identity is based on social and cultural identifiers. This acknowledgment brought into question the principle of hypodescent, which assigns children of a mixed race to the less privileged group. The classification choices, however, left intact the idea that white and black are racial rather than ethnic categories. The federal government designated the white majority not by a label designed specifically for them, but by referring to what they were not.

People of multiple racial and ethnic origins have started a social movement, and over the last few decades several groups have been formed. The most powerful has been the Association of Multiethnic Americans, which was founded in 1988. This association coordinates several different organizations to orchestrate strategies for an official recognition of multiracial identifiers and has challenged negative images of mixed-race couples (Hollinger, 2003). Members of the collaborative agree that they should not be defined on the basis of biological notions of race. This association was instrumental in the changes in the last census, which allowed individuals to pick several categories instead of one.

Ethnoracial Diversity

Within each ethnoracial group in the United States there is great variability. When people think of major ethnoracial groups in the United States, they conceive of these groups as a homogenous whole consisting of individuals who have the same attributes and politics. This is convenient but problematic, because this belief allows people to disregard the diversity within these groups and the similarities between them. This way of thinking supports cultural imperialism, in which one group defines itself as normal and from this position establishes the values and norms by which everyone is judged.

The U.S. Census Bureau currently lists the following ethnoracial groups: Hispanic or Latino, Asian, Native Hawaiian and other Pacific Islander, black or African American, American Indian and Alaska Native, and white. There is also an "other" category that respondents may select. Within each of these groups multiple parameters of difference exist. Variation occurs as a result of many factors, including country of origin, language, class and income, and history of incorporation into the United States. The only groups whose ancestors did not come to the United States as refugees or other immigrants are obviously Native Americans, Native Alaskans, and Native Hawaiians.

The more than 35 million Latino/Latina people in the United States vary widely by country of origin, language, class and income, and immigration history. The vast majority of those in the United States within this group come from Spanish-speaking countries (see table 3.1). Some, however, come from

TABLE 3.1   Population of Latino/Latina Groups in the United States, 2000

Mexican	20,900,102
Puerto Rican	3,403,510
Cuban	1,249,820
Central American (from Costa Rica, Guatemala, Honduras, Nicaragua, Panama, Salvador)	1,811,676
South American (from Argentina, Bolivia, Columbia, Ecuador, Paraguay, Peru, Uruguay, Venezuela)	1,419,979
Dominican	799,768
Spanish	112,999
Other	5,540,627

Source: U.S. Census Bureau (2004). *We the people: Hispanics in the United States.* Retrieved January 2, 2008, from http://www.census.gov/prod/2004pubs/censr-18.pdf

Portuguese-speaking countries. In addition, some of the indigenous people from Latin America speak one or more of many indigenous languages. In Mexico alone there are approximately sixty-two indigenous languages. Approximately 58.5 percent of Latinos and Latinas in the United States are of Mexican ancestry. Almost 10 percent identify as Puerto Rican, and 3.5 percent as Cuban. Another 9.7 percent come from Central American countries, and 6.4 percent from South American countries (U.S. Census Bureau, 2004c).

Many Latinos/Latinas in the United States who were born in other countries have lost or partially lost the language of their country of origin. Each ethnoracial group has characteristics that arise from its unique history. Among Latinos, many Mexican immigrants came from dirt farms and small villages, while many Cuban Americans fleeing Castro were middle class. Most Puerto Ricans on the U.S. mainland, who are not immigrants at all since Puerto Rico is a commonwealth of the United States, come from cities in Puerto Rico. Many lived in the crowded and impoverished urban neighborhoods of San Juan and now live in northeastern U.S. cities (Levine, 2003).

Even more diversity exists among the more than 11 million people of Asian ancestry in the United States (see table 3.2). Chinese Americans, of whom there are almost 2.5 million, make up the largest group. Groups of Filipino, Asian Indian, Vietnamese, and Korean heritage consist of more than a million individuals each, while there are fewer than a million Japanese Americans (U.S. Census Bureau, 2001, 2004b). There is no umbrella language that unites all these groups, and while each group has its own distinctive culture, there are still many cultural variations within each group (Levine, 2003). Since the mid-1960s Asian Americans have been viewed by much of society as the model community of color. This sounds positive, but this belief has been damaging. Tong (2000) makes the argument that because of this belief, the hardships that have been experienced by Asian families and communities are ignored. More people in Chinese American families than in white families work; this is why many Chinese American families have higher family incomes. However, in 1990, 11 percent of

TABLE 3.2   Population of Asian American Groups and Pacific Islanders in the United States, 2000

Chinese	2,422,970
Filipino	1,864,120
Asian Indian	1,645,510
Vietnamese	1,110,207
Korean	1,072,682
Japanese	795,051
Cambodian	178,043
Hmong	170,049
Laotian	167,792
Pakistani	155,909
Thai	110,851
Other Asian	478,636
Native Hawaiian and other Pacific Islander	874,414

Source: U.S. Census Bureau (2001). *The Native Hawaiian and other Pacific Islander population: 2000.* Retrieved September 2, 2007, from http://www.census.gov/prod/2001pubs/c2kbr01-14.pdf; U.S. Census Bureau (2004). *We the people: Asians in the United States.* Retrieved September 2, 2007, from http://www.census.gov/prod/2004pubs/censr-17.pdf

Chinese American families lived in poverty, and in 2000 the number was 14 percent. While only 3 percent of the total U.S. population in 2000 was Asian American, it is estimated that this population will continue to grow in the future. The projection is that this group will grow at a rate of 3.8 percent per year, reaching nearly 22 million by 2025. Native Hawaiians and other Pacific Islander populations are recognized as a group in the census but are often categorized with Asian Americans. These groups total approximately half the population of Japanese Americans and are made up of people from Hawaii, Guam, Samoa, and other Pacific Islands.

The 36,213,467 people who identify as black or African American make up approximately 12.3 percent of the U.S. population (see table 3.3). Many African Americans are of West African ancestry; however, there is little recognition of the diversity of their history in terms of the languages and countries of origin of their ancestors. There are also more than a million West Indian Americans, including people from Jamaica and Haiti. In addition, the population from sub-Saharan Africa is growing (Pulera, 2002; U.S. Census Bureau, 2004a).

TABLE 3.3   Population of Blacks in the United States, 2000

African American	33,792,201
Caribbean	1,420,933
African	571,021
Central and South American	312,549
Other	116,703

Source: U.S. Census Bureau (2005). *We the people: Blacks in the United States.* Retrieved January 13, 2008, at http://www.census.gov/prod/2005pubs/censr-25.pdf.

The ethnoracial grouping of Native Americans and Native Alaskan people consists of the indigenous peoples of the continental United States and Alaska. There is great diversity within this group (see table 3.4). This group now numbers approximately 2.5 million people, only 1.5 percent of the total population, which is a tragedy beyond comprehension. It is estimated that there were 50 to 100 million indigenous people in North America in 1492. There are 569 federally recognized tribes, as well as a number that are not recognized. It is estimated that about half of this population lives outside the reservations (Center for Disease Control, n.d.).

TABLE 3.4   Population of Selected Native American and Native Alaskan Tribes in the United States, 2000

Apache	96,833
Cherokee	729,533
Chippewa	149,669
Choctaw	158,774
Creek	71,310
Iroquois	80,822
Lumbee	57,868
Navajo	298,197
Pueblo	74,085
Sioux	153,360
Eskimo	54,761
Alaska Athabascan	18,838

Source: U.S. Census Bureau (2006). *The American Indian and Alaska Native population: 2000* Retrieved September 2, 2007, from http://www.census.gov/prod/2002pubs/c2kbr01-15.pdf

Almost 200 million people self-identify as white (see table 3.5). Within this group, people have different ancestries. Most are of German, Irish and English ancestry (U.S. Census Bureau, 2004a). Poor whites, particularly those living in rural areas, are stigmatized and viewed as the "other" (Roediger, 2002). The use of derogatory terms creates isolation and shame. Due to their social and economic conditions, they are outside powered relations. Access to education is often limited, and this situation provides a basis for stratification within white groups. Those living in poor white rural communities are often labeled "backward." People with Appalachian roots are one group that struggles with the stigma and shame connected to poverty-based isolation.

Immigration

Immigration accounts for the largest percentage of population growth in the United States. Immigrants continue to transform the social ambience, culture, and politics of the country. As of the 2000 census, immigrants constituted more than 10 percent of the nation's population (U.S. Census Bureau, 2000a).

TABLE 3.5   Population of Selected White Ethnic Groups in the United States, 2000

German	42,841,569
Irish	30,524,799
English	24,509,692
Italian	15,638,348
French	8,309,666
Polish	8,977,235
Dutch	4,541,770
Scotch Irish	4,319,232
Scottish	4,890,581
Swedish	3,998,310
Norwegian	4,477,725
Russian	2,652,214
Welsh	1,753,794

Source: U.S. Census Bureau (2004). *Ancestry: 2000.* Retrieved January 2, 2008, from http://www.census.gov/prod/2004pubs/c2kbr-35.pdf

Together, immigrants of color, along with their U.S.-born children, constitute one-fifth of the population in the United States. In 2000, that was 56 million people (Foner, 2003). In 2002 almost 23 percent of children born in the United States had a mother who was born outside the United States. This is the largest percent since the early 1900s. Many of those born in earlier years were born of mothers from Italy and eastern Europe. Today, many of these mothers are Latina, who account for 59 percent of immigrant births. Close to 10 percent of U.S.-born children have mothers who were born in Mexico. Conservative factions frame this shift as impending doom for white American culture and identity (Buchanan, 2002). Foner (2003) writes that "If today's foreign born and their children were to form a country, it would have approximately twice the population of Canada and roughly the same as France or Italy" (p. 30). This is considered the second-greatest wave of immigration that the United States has experienced. The first occurred at the turn of the twentieth century. These new immigrants are from all over the world, and they are mainly non-European. Since the 1980s, more than 85 percent of the immigrants admitted to the United States have come from the Americas and Asia, while only 10 percent have come from Europe. People of color from Africa, the Caribbean, and the Middle East have also immigrated, but in lower numbers. As they join social groups that have historically been targets of racism and ethnicism, their reception is negatively affected by the five mechanisms of oppression.

While immigrant groups from Latin America, Africa, Asia, and Europe all play a significant role in the growth and development of the United States, public debate is currently focused on Latino/Latina immigrants. There are several reasons for this, the first of which are the large number of Latino/Latina immigrants and the proximity of their home countries. This group accounts for the majority of current immigrants, most of whom (27.7% of U.S. immigrants) come from

Mexico, followed by those from Central and South America. This focus, coupled with institutionalized racism, serves to mobilize public fear. Further, due to their proximity, it is easy for immigrants to move between countries, maintaining the language and culture of their native country. This, however, is becoming increasingly difficult with new immigration laws. Ironically, this situation has resulted in increased numbers of immigrants because it has become more difficult for migrants to move freely across the U.S.-Mexican border. In addition, in the past, Latino/Latina immigrants (both documented and undocumented) have been primarily concentrated in California, Texas, New York, Florida, Illinois, Arizona, and New Jersey, where almost 80 percent currently live. Increasingly, however, Latinos/Latinas are spreading to other areas, including Georgia, Maryland, North Carolina, Pennsylvania, Virginia, Tennessee, and Minnesota (Center for Immigration Studies, 2001). In 2005, there were approximately 15,000 Mexicans in Hawaii and 20,000 in Alaska ("Mexicans Spreading Out," 2005).

One of the most controversial issues in the immigration debate is illegal immigration. The word "illegal" has been challenged. Framing undocumented workers as illegal makes them "by definition criminal" (India, 2006, p. 64). Many Latinos/Latinas are offended by the use of the words "alien" and "illegal" to describe undocumented immigrants, who only "want the same thing all Americans do, which is adequate food, shelter, and clothing," and prefer "the term *undocumented worker* or at the very least *unauthorized immigrants*" (Acuña, 2003, p. 72). There are varying estimates of the number of undocumented immigrants in the United States. According to the Pew Hispanic Center, in 2005 there were 10 million undocumented immigrants (Johnson, 2006). Johnson estimates that of the 10 million, 56 percent are from Mexico, 24 percent from other Latin American countries, 10 percent from Asia, 6 percent from Europe and Canada, and 4 percent from other countries. Other estimates place the number as high as 20 million (Eibel, 2007). Although Latinos and Latinas were in this country when Plymouth Rock was, as Korrol (1996) says, "just a pebble," and have experienced oppression since that time, that oppression has been exacerbated by the anti-immigration debate.

The intersecting oppression of racism and oppression based on nationality are intensified by poverty for many refugees and other immigrants. While some immigrants from Latin America—both legal and undocumented—are rapidly moving into the middle and upper classes, many remain in low-paid jobs and continue to live in poverty. According to Bean, Trejo, Capps, and Tyler (2001), the Latino middle class in the United States is made up of about 2.7 million households, which is about 12 million people. This is about 33 percent of all Latinos. The majority of immigrants, however, were poor in their country of origin and remain poor in the United States. These groups tend to be the new "servant class." They fill many of the labor positions in the garment industry, restaurants, farms, and parking garages, landscaping, and painting (Shipler, 2004). Only about 4.4 percent come to the United States with a college degree (Center for Immigration Studies, 2001), and undocumented immigrants tend to be poorly educated: "Among 25–64 year olds, almost half are not high school graduates. As a result—and despite very high labor force participation for men—wages and incomes are low. Nationwide, in 2003, 27% of adult illegal immigrants and 39% of illegal children lived in poverty" (Johnson, 2006, p. 5).

Asian immigrants total around 10 million people. The largest number are from China, followed by those from the Philippines, Japan, India, Korea, Vietnam, Laos, and Cambodia (Segal, 2002). Today, "the Asian born are the country's second largest foreign-born population by world region of birth behind those from Latin America" (Dixon, 2006). This group, like Latinos/Latinas, has been the target of racism, which has exposed them to Young's five faces of oppression (exploitation, marginalization, powerlessness, cultural imperialism, and violence). For many years, the Chinese Exclusion Act prohibited Asians from entering the United States. Even though this group has the highest rate of immigrants who are professionals and is seen as the "model" group of color, 14 percent of the population is poor (Rodgers, 2000). The concept of the model minority has been used to chide other groups of color in the United States for not doing better and implies that Asian Americans no longer suffer from the decades of marginalization experienced by this group (Bascara, 2001).

The current wave of black immigrants comes from the West Indies and Africa. West Indian immigrants include individuals from the Bahamas, Barbados, Belize, Bermuda, Guyana, Jamaica, Trinidad, and Tobago (Denmark, Eisberg, Heitner, & Holder, 2003). The 2000 census documented around 250,000 black immigrants from Africa. These immigrants experience the racial oppression blacks have historically faced in the United States. Too often, ethnoracially white groups do not differentiate between black African and African American groups. However, some resentments surface among African Americans who feel that these newcomers experience fewer obstacles based on race than they themselves do.

Immigrants from the Middle East come from countries such as Pakistan, Saudi Arabia, Israel, Turkey, and Iraq (Camarota, 2003). In 1970 there were around 200,000 individuals of Middle Eastern descent living in the United States; at the time of the 2000 census there were 1.5 million. This group was the target of racism well before the September 11, 2001, attack on the World Trade Center in New York City. After this tragedy, the belief that all Arabs are Muslim and all Muslims are Arab, and that this group wants to wage a holy war on the United States, became widespread, and a general hostility toward Arabs and Muslims spread.

Class

Examination of cultures and differences within each group reveals class differences. In the United States, the full extent of class differences is commonly denied. Many people claim to be middle class, even if their income is significantly lower or higher, and assets fewer or greater, than those in this socioeconomic class. The reality is that we all live in very separate economic worlds. In the United States, contrary to popular belief, economic groupings are racialized.

While there is no agreement on how these groupings of class structure look, Gilbert has developed a model that is used by many but it is not without controversy. This model provides a comprehensive picture and identifies six classes:

1. The capitalistic class is comprised of high-level politicians, heirs, and top-level executives who typically have prestigious university educations and annual family incomes over $325,000.
2. The upper-middle class consists of upper managers, professionals, and midsized-business owners with a college education, most often with an advanced degree, who have family incomes between $100,000 and $325,000.
3. The lower-middle class consists of semi-professionals and skilled crafts-people who usually have attended some college or possess a college degree and earn family incomes of about $50,000–100,000.
4. The working class is composed of clerical workers, assembly and factory workers, and other blue-collar employees, who generally have high school degrees and family incomes of about $25,000–50,000.
5. The working poor are service workers and laborers and clerical workers in low-wage sectors who usually did not graduate from high school and have family incomes of approximately $15,000–25,000.
6. The poor or "underclass" are people who are unemployed or only able to find seasonal or part-time work and are dependent on temporary or informal employment or some form of social assistance; they generally have family incomes under $15,000 (Gilbert, 2002; U.S. Census Bureau, 2007).

In 2004, 12.7 percent (37 million) of people in the United States lived in poverty. African Americans, Native Americans/Native Alaskans, and Latinos suffer higher rates of poverty than whites and Asians. Blacks and Native Americans/Native Alaskans have the highest poverty rates: 24.7 percent for blacks, and 25 percent for Native Americans/Native Alaskans. The poverty rate for Latinos is 21.9 percent. The poverty rate among Asians and Pacific Islanders is 9.8 percent, and among non-Latino/Latina whites, the poverty rate is the lowest: 8.6 percent (U.S. Census Bureau, 2005c). Even though the poverty rate for whites is lower than for other groups, because whites make up the largest share of the population, they account for nearly half of those living in poverty.

Individuals, families, and communities living in poverty often become the providers of menial labor. The interaction between poverty and racism results in the assumption that members of oppressed groups should serve those of the privileged group (Young, 2000). For example, many positions in the fast-food industry are held by people of color. The median pay is $10,482 per year, with no benefits (U.S. Census Bureau, 2005b). Domestic work in the United States is also racialized. A 2003–2004 survey in New York found that 95 percent of domestic workers were people of color (Domestic Workers United & DataCenter, 2006). Twenty-six percent of these workers are paid wages below the poverty level (less than $9.00 per hour), while 41 percent earn $9.00–13.00 per hour; most aren't paid overtime (Domestic Workers United & DataCenter, 2006). Further, in 1999, classified ads in the *Los Angeles Times* advertised for nannies and house-keepers willing to work for wages starting as low as $100 to $125 per week (Hondagneu-Sotelo, 2001). Migrant farmworkers in the United States provide another example of racialized exploitation. It is estimated that 75 percent of the 3 million farmworkers in the United States are from Mexico (U.S. Department of Labor, 2005). In 2000–2001, farmworkers averaged $10,000–12,499 a year; 30 percent were below the poverty level (U.S. Department of Labor, 2005). Less than 10 percent of migrant workers are white.

The Intersection of Race/Ethnicity, Class, and Gender

Examination of the multiple categories people occupy (or are relegated to), including race/ethnicity, gender/sex, class, national origin, sexual orientation, and ability, reveals the complexity and compounds our understanding of the mechanisms of oppression. These categories, as well as others, can constitute separate forms of disadvantage. But individuals who occupy more than one of these categories experience the intersection of oppressions as well (Delgado & Stefancic, 2001).

Without understanding that various statuses and structures intersect to create what Frye (2000) refers to as a cage, we cannot see the constraints that hold people in place, preventing them from exercising their full potential. When race and ethnicity are used to determine who has access to goods and services, when gender and sex, ability, and/or sexual orientation are used to determine worthiness, and when parental status is used to determine professional and economic risk, we rob people of the right to determine their own fate.

Case studies such as the one in box 3.1 help to illustrate these intersections. Yolanda experiences discrimination based on the intersections of multiple oppressions of sexism, racism, and bias against single parents. Because George has not examined his assumptions, Yolanda is an undesirable loan risk in his eyes, even though she is financially solvent and well educated. Thus in her interactions with George, Yolanda experiences four of the five faces of oppression. Often, both the oppressed and the oppressor fail to recognize oppression.

Box 3.1 *Yolanda's Home Mortgage*

Yolanda is hoping to buy her first home. As a woman of color who is also a single mother, she experiences multiple forms of oppression that are unique to her and other women in the same position. Yolanda experiences oppression because of her race, because of her gender, and because she is a single parent. When she goes to her local bank to inquire about a home mortgage loan, she encounters a loan officer who is less than helpful. Before he denies her loan, the loan officer, George, tries to dissuade her from considering a home mortgage. Yolanda senses a dismissive tone in him. George feels that she is a poor loan risk even though she is college educated and in a professional position, earns a good wage, has a good credit rating, and has had uninterrupted employment for the last seven years. Yolanda wonders if she is being denied the loan because she is a woman, because she is a woman of color, because she is a single parent, or if it is the combination of the three.

Yolanda knows of white couples, single black men, and single white women who have been able to obtain home mortgages from this bank. In fact, she has heard that George tends to go out of his way to help customers. Unfortunately, George has worked with neither women of color nor single parents. But he has read about single mothers struggling to make ends meet in his local newspaper. Consequently, his vision is clouded by the assumption that, as a single mother, Yolanda must be struggling. Instead of reviewing her application on its own merits, George makes assumptions regarding its viability based on her overlapping group identities.

Individuals and communities of color experience Young's five faces of oppression. People of color face economic exploitation and marginalization due to structural barriers embedded into the political, social, and economic systems. Likewise, they experience the frustrations of overlapping systems that work to keep them powerless, and the cultural imperialism that frames them as the "other."

Chapter 4

Gender, Sexual Orientation, and Sex

> The emotional, sexual, and psychological stereotyping of females begins when the doctor says: "It's a girl."
>
> Shirley Chisholm

Understanding the creation of gender identity and the development of sexual orientation requires us to accept the multifaceted experience of sex and gender. We are taught that sex and gender are synonymous, and that only one of two options is assigned at birth. Socialization occurs based on that assignment. We grow up socialized to gender roles, and we come to understand that male is better than female and that we are all supposed to be heterosexual. This is assumed to be natural, and these beliefs are implicit in our norms. Failure to follow gender role expectations, including those dictating the gender of those with whom we engage in sexual and romantic relationships, is considered unnatural and labeled deviant. Although gender is assumed to arise from sex, gender and the roles that are assigned to each gender are inherently socially and culturally based (Greene, 2000).

Many labels can be applied to the mechanisms that enforce gendered oppression—sexism, heterosexism, homophobia. Sexism, homophobia, and heterosexism are powerful social forces that affect all social groups. Sexism, the preferential treatment of males over females, and misogyny, the hatred of females and femininity, underlie the oppression of individuals who are female, gender variant, or transgender as well as those who are gay, lesbian, and bisexual.

Homophobia, the fear of and hostility toward gay and lesbian people, is a product of sexism and reinforces gender role expectations. Heterosexism, the assumption that everyone is and should be heterosexual, contributes to the stigma attached to individuals who do not conform to societal gender norm expectations. Heterosexist attitudes, or heterocentrism, are subtler and less visible than homophobia in the same way that white privilege is less visible than overt racism. It is harder to name, uncover, address, and, thus, change. These mind-sets are developed and maintained through education, socialization, and language. They are reinforced by the games of young children (Szegedy-Maszak, 2001). A boy who is not willing to engage in the aggressive games and behavior that are expected of boys may be referred to as a "girl" or a "sissy," labels that suggest inferiority of the boy in question as well as all females and are often used to demean people who are lesbian or gay. "One of the social functions of the persecution of 'the sissy' is to force other boys into gender role compliance" (Brooks, 2000, p. 108). Boys as well as girls who do not comply face isolation and persecution.

Oppressions in the United States are interlocking, mutually reinforcing, and based on dynamics of domination and subordination (Jenson, 1998). Lorde (1983) writes that "Oppression and the intolerance of difference come in all shapes and sizes and colors and sexualities. . . . If we truly intend to eliminate oppression and achieve human liberation, heterosexism and homophobia must be addressed" (p. 9). The oppression of individuals and communities is intertwined in their complexities. Gender, sex, and sexual orientation overlap, and people's experiences of these identities are made more complex by race/ethnicity, ability, class, age, nationality, and religion.

Gender and Sex

While the myth is that all people are either male or female, in actuality this is not the case. Gender is more than physical biology, and it is not a dichotomous phenomenon that defines an individual as either masculine or feminine (Fausto-Sterling, 1992; Garnets, 2002). It is a social construction that is shaped by social and cultural context. Gender roles are learned and interact with social structures (Bryson, 1999; Butler, 1999). These social structures reinforce the inequality of women, and this is supported by patriarchal systems of male dominance. Although the terms "sex" and "gender" are generally used interchangeably, there is a clear difference between the two. Gender is the social construct related to the roles, behaviors, and attitudes we expect from people based on their categorization as male or female, while sex refers to the biological designation of male and female (based primarily on reproductive organs). However, according to Bryson (1999), "Even at the level of biological difference, the basis for a binary division between men and women does not exist" (p. 49). At birth, individuals are legally classified as male or female. At that point, a whole set of gender expectations is mapped onto this primary sex distinction (Bryson, 1999). An individual's internal sense of gender is her or his gender identity. This was once presumed to be a dichotomous choice—masculine and feminine; however, we are now beginning to understand gender as a continuum rather than as a dichotomy. A person may identify her- or himself as female or male, or as intersexual or transgender (Boston Women's Health Book Collective, 1998).

The term "intersex" refers to a diverse group of individuals who are born with genetic and chromosomal anomalies, and people with so-called ambiguous genitalia. For example, some individuals are born with an XXXY chromosomal configuration, which means they have both male and female reproductive organs. Some are born with genitalia that appear to be in between male and female. Too often surgery is performed on intersex infants before medical tests identifying sex can be conducted and the implications for the child as she or he matures can be considered. Parents of intersex children are frequently isolated and ill informed and have no medical or community support. Box 4.1 tells the story of an intersex individual.

Box 4.1   I Am Both Female and Male

I grew up a boy, socialized to a man's profession. An engineer, I am successful in a "man's world." I design and contract out large projects. I married a woman as quiet as I am talkative. By the time I was twenty-two years of age, I had a son. I loved my wife deeply and we both believed in lifetime commitments.

Imagine my (our) surprise when I became ill, a life-threatening illness that baffled many experts. The diagnosis? Puberty—that is, my second puberty . . . puberty as a woman. This is what almost killed me. Unbeknownst to me or the doctors, I was menstruating internally and ended up with a terrible infection. While I was hospitalized for the infection, they discovered I had a uterus. I couldn't believe it. The feelings were overwhelming: fear, disbelief, grief, confusion.

Although the hospital social worker in our small city did not know much about intersex people or issues, she was compassionate and open. She took the time to explore the biological and social issues and found support and educational resources for my wife and me. The social worker provided information for the health professionals while also helping me and my wife through the crisis. I decided not to remove my uterus; instead I now manage the two sexes with hormones. In time, we had a second child and I am now going through menopause.

Over the years I have done a lot of reading and personal reflection. Because of my family and my career, I have chosen to live in the world as a man, and the world around me considers me a man. What I have come to recognize, however, is that internally, I identify as a woman—a woman in love with a woman. So, in many ways, my true identity remains hidden from those I love. Only my wife knows, and she considers herself to be married to a man. There was some sadness in my decision not to tell others, but we worried about the impact that would have on our children. Now, I am beginning to share my identity and life experience with others.

Transgender is a label that is currently in transition. Historically, it has been used as a catchall term to describe multiple categories, including transsexuals (individuals who experience gender dysphoria, that is, those whose physical anatomy does not conform to their internal sense of themselves as male or female) and people who are intersex. Because individuals who have historically been labeled transsexual now prefer the term "transgender," or the abbreviated term "trans," for self-identification, the word "transgender" will be used in this text to refer to people whose sexual anatomy at birth does not match their internal sense of their own gender. With the advances that have taken place in medical science since the early 1950s, it has become possible for transgender individuals to go through hormonal treatments and have their anatomy altered through sexual reassignment surgery, sometimes called gender reassignment surgery. However, only a small minority of people whose genitalia is inconsistent with their own sense of their gender seek sexual reassignment surgery (Wren, 2000). It is important to realize that gender identity and sexual orientation are not necessarily connected. Transgender and intersex people may identify as gay, straight, or bisexual, and gender reassignment surgery may or may not change an individual's identification of sexual orientation.

Transgenderphobia, or transphobia, is the fear and hatred of transgender people. It is similar to homophobia and is a major threat to the safety and well-being of transgender populations (Mallon, 1999b, 1999c). Like homophobia, transphobia falls along a continuum ranging from disapproval to violence. Transgender people of color are most likely to experience violence and most murders of transgender people occur as a result of racism, sexism, and transphobia, meaning that most transgender murder victims are trans women of color (Bettcher, 2007; Lombardi & Bettcher, 2005).

The Social Construction of Gender Roles

Gender roles, or the belief that certain roles are appropriate for women and men, are socially constructed (Burr, 1995). The assignment of labels of "masculine" and "feminine" to every aspect of human behavior results in rigid expectations that affect both females and males. There are consequences for individuals who exhibit gender-variant behavior, that is, behavior that falls outside the bounds of what has been identified as masculine or feminine based on social assumptions and traditions. Those who violate the rules and regulations that govern gender roles by not conforming are often ostracized, marginalized, stigmatized, and mistreated (Bem, 1993).

The question is what should be done now with gender and sex roles. Fausto-Sterling (1992), a biologist, argues that there are "very few absolute sex differences and that without complete social equality we cannot know for sure what they are" (pp. 269–270). Risman (1998) argues that "gendered expectations in American families are major impediments to further movement towards equality" (p. 151). She asks, "If we are to allow individuals full room to maneuver, to build on their strengths, to create themselves, why shackle any of us with cognitive images that restrict us to gendered notions? Why differentiate at all in the way we socialize girls and boys? . . . My answer is that gender should be irrelevant to all aspects of our lives" (p. 157).

Both feminist literature and studies on boys emphasize the harmful effects that the enforcement of rigid gender roles have on children. Pollack and Shuster (2000) call it the "gender straightjacket" (p. 9) and lament that "society is pushing them to be just one kind of person, nudging them at a very young age to disconnect from their loved ones and to sacrifice that part within themselves that is genuinely loving, caring, and affectionate" (p. 5). Pipher (1994) describes a similar fate for adolescent girls, a culture that splits adolescent girls into "true and false selves. The culture is what causes girls to abandon their true selves and take up false selves" (p. 37). She calls our culture "girl-poisoning" (p. 28). It is frightening to realize how toxic this culture is for both boys and girls who feel that they must amputate parts of their emotional selves to survive in their social environments.

As early as preschool, children participate in the institutionalization of gender "appropriate" behavior. If a boy tries to play at cooking with the girls, at least one of the girls is likely to turn him away, chastising him for trying to play a girl's game (Szegedy-Maszak, 2001). The more children are allowed to segregate by gender, the less interested they are in breaking stereotypes (Szegedy-Maszak, 2001).

Gender-variant children suffer early on as a result of social labeling; these negative consequences serve to perpetuate rigid gender expectations. "Sissy" is a popular term for boys who act in what would be considered feminine ways. As a derogatory term, it is used to denigrate boys and men who behave in gender-nonconforming ways. Sissies occupy a stigmatized and vulnerable social position and are usually considered social misfits, especially by other boys (Brooks, 2000; Corbett, 1999; Mallon, 1999c). "Tomboy" is a popular term for gender-variant girls and has a wider range of meanings than "sissy." "Tomboy" can be used as a derogatory or complimentary label. Since it is often socially acceptable to be a tomboy, it is important to contrast the differential treatment of boys who "act like girls" from girls who "act like boys." This occurs as a result of sexist attitudes that underlie the assumption that male is better than female.

The case for lessening or even eliminating gender roles is becoming increasingly strong. According to Cook (1985), "It is widely believed today that strict adherence to sex-appropriate standards for characteristics and behavior can adversely affect the psychological well-being of both sexes" (p. 152). Garbarino (1999) writes that androgyny is one of the major foundations for resilience in young boys: "The more successfully people incorporate both traditionally masculine and traditionally feminine attributes, the more likely they are to master the situations they face" (p. 169).

Gendered Oppression

Discrimination against women is widespread, and the violation of the rights of women occurs on many levels on a daily basis. Many females are exposed to gender-based violence in the home and the community. The disadvantages experienced by women are created by and maintained through cultural beliefs and stereotypes that present narrow, distorted, and harmful images of women (Milkie, 2002).

The media assists in promoting and maintaining disadvantages faced by women by ignoring, trivializing, and distorting information about them. Images that prescribe what women should do, be like, or look like are powerful yet subtle vehicles of control. These images play a significant role in defining gender roles through everyday practices and discourses. They have profound negative effects on all populations.

Sexism describes the social, economic, and political system established to maintain power relationships that privilege men over women. Sexism is tied to the concept of patriarchy, "a social system in which structural differences in privilege, power, and authority are invested in masculinity" (Cranny-Francis, Waring, Stauropoulos, & Kirby, 2003, p. 15). Patriarchal power structures serve to keep white men in dominant and privileged positions. Patriarchal oppression is maintained through the manipulation of individual identity as well as structural, social, economic, and political systems (Bryson, 1999; Saulnier, 2000). Gender classifications are used to justify the denial of opportunities to women that are provided to men (Bryson, 1999). These justifications support the assumptions that give rise to gender roles that are seen as unchangeable (Moi, 1999).

Economics and Demographics

"Women represent half of the planet's population, but account for the 70% of the 1.3 billion people who live below the poverty level" (World March, 2000). In the United States, women make up 51 percent of the population. They are more likely to live in poverty than men (U.S. Census Bureau, 2000b). The low wages of women result in the higher rates of poverty experienced by female-headed households (Schmitz & Tebb, 1999). In the United States, female-headed families experienced a poverty rate (26.5%) more than five times that of two-parent families (4.9%), and almost twice that of male-headed single-parent families (13.6%) (U.S. Census Bureau, 2002). The rates of poverty are particularly high for female-headed families of color (see table 4.1).

Although race and ethnicity have historically been conceptualized as gender neutral, there are clear trends running counter to this view (Handrahan, 2002). Women and men both suffer from discrimination based on race, ethnicity, and country of origin. These experiences differ according to gender. These

TABLE 4.1 Poverty Rates by Family Type and Race/Ethnicity, 2001

Race/Ethnicity	Female Headed	Male Headed	Two Parent
Total	26.5%	13.6%	4.9%
White non-Latino	19%	10.3%	3.3%
Black	35.2%	19.4%	7.8%
Asian and Pacific Islanders	14.6%	9.1%	6.6%
Latino	37%	17%	13.8%

Source: U.S. Census Bureau (2002). *Poverty in the United States: 2001.* Washington, DC: U.S. Government Printing Office.

intersecting oppressions are referred to as racialized gender or gendered ethnicity (Crenshaw, 1995; Glenn, 1992).Women of color—African American, Native American, Latina, and Asian American—are some of the poorest groups in
the United States.White women tend to earn more money than women of color
in part because they tend to be able to stay in school longer than women of
color. However, even when education is controlled for, women of color experience higher rates of poverty (Caiazza, Shaw, & Werschkul, 2004).

Women are both divided by and interconnected by race, class, and national
origin.Women of color make up a large part of the "servant class" in the United
States (Ehrenreich, 2002). In 2006 the U.S. Department of Labor reported that
32.8 percent of domestic workers in private homes were Latina, while 11.1 percent were black and 2.5 percent were Asian.The median income for these workers in 2006 was $355 a week, $41 below the poverty level for a family of four.

As women in wealthy countries move into the workplace, women from
poor nations migrate to fill the labor gap in care roles.The result is a gap in female labor and care back home (Ehrenreich & Hochschild, 2002). Much of this
labor shift is racialized, as the women who travel to serve the needs of white individuals, families, and communities are women of color.

Feminism: A Movement for Change

Feminism is about ending all oppression, including gendered oppression. More
specifically, it is "a) a belief that women all over the world face some form of oppression or exploitation, b) a commitment to uncover and understand what
causes and sustains oppression, and c) a commitment to work individually and
collectively in everyday life to end all forms of oppression, whether based on
gender, class, race or culture" (Maguire, 1987, p. 5). It is not anti-male. Nor is it a
white women's movement, as it has been called by some critics. Neither sexism
nor feminism inherently belongs to any particular gender. Individuals of any
gender or sex can be sexist; likewise, individuals of any gender or sex can be
feminist.

African American women have been major contributors to the development of feminist theory (Brewer, 1993; Saulnier, 2000).Women are, however, divided by the different worldviews created by race, class, and sexual orientation.
Although these different worldviews have created blinders and divisions, they
also have the potential to add depth to the women's movement. Too often,
white women are "unaware of their own experience of race or the privileges
accorded to them as members of the dominant group" (Saulnier, 2000, p. 16). As
a result, it can be hard for them to understand the importance of race and the
impact of racism.

Race cannot be separated from gender, class, or sexual orientation. African
American feminists who have theorized about the juncture of race and gender
were joined in theorizing by other women of color in the 1970s and 1980s
(White, 2001). Black women have helped to emphasize the significance of class

in feminist analysis. "Most centrally, black feminists are concerned by the negative impact that interactions between categories of identity, such as sexuality, race, class and gender, have on black women's lives" (White, 2001, p. 80). Black intellectuals have also increased our awareness of the connection between race and sexuality.

"Feminism defined as a movement to end sexist oppression enables women and men, girls and boys, to participate equally in revolutionary struggle" (hooks, 1984, p. 67). Early feminism from the mid-nineteenth century to the early twentieth century (often called first wave feminism) was characterized by anti-male bias and excluded not only males as allies, but also many women of color and women in poverty who had to chose between feminism and their own communities (hooks, 1984). Too often, women of color were caught between sexism in their own communities and anti-male racist feminist movements. The patriarchal attitudes of the anti-racist black movement and the racial blindness of the anti-sexist women's movement severely limited the ability of African American women to address their own concerns (Crenshaw, 1990). The social position of African American women is structured in the interaction of power hierarchies (Dawson, 2001). Their experience of oppression at the intersection of race and sex/gender is neither parallel nor simply additive. The intersection creates a new oppression, that of women of color. Simplistic thinking that focuses on either one or the other form of oppression as primary fails to recognize, honor, and address the complexity of this experience. In failing to understand that one cannot view just one or the other as the primary oppression in society, neither early anti-racist nor feminist movements adequately addressed the forms of disadvantage faced by women of color. Both movements dismissed the claims of black women as peripheral. Other women of color have experienced similar exclusions.

The liberal feminism of the 1970s, second wave feminism, was based on the sociopolitical concerns of middle-class heterosexual white women (Saulnier, 2000). The most oppressed—women of color, women in poverty, women without children, lesbian and bisexual women—were never consulted (hooks, 1984). Third wave feminism, which includes cultural, postmodern, womanist, and radical feminism, has emerged since then (see Saulnier, 2000, for a more thorough discussion). Each has brought new depth and a broader lens to feminism. Cultural feminists work to eliminate the divisions separating women, including racism, while firmly supporting the profound differences between women and men. Cultural feminism, which views women as closer than men to nature, grew out of radical feminism (Echols, 1998). Postmodern feminists recognize the power of language and the impact of language on the social construction of gender (Butler, 1999). Gender is recognized as contextualized in culture, language, and time.

Womanism, which focuses on the experiences of women of color, developed in response to feminism's failure to address the concerns of women of color (Collins, 1996; Grant, 1995). The philosophy of womanism views gender, race, and class as forming a single consciousness requiring an integrated response to sexism, racism, and classism (Riggs, 1994). According to Saulnier (2000), "Womanism starts with the perspective of black women rather than white men and centers on the *complex matrix* of oppression" (p. 17). Racial consciousness underscores the positives of African American life and focuses on social change and self-healing.

Radical feminism regards patriarchy as the system of oppression that subordinates women, and it seeks to overthrow that system. Radical feminists view societal institutions such as family, heterosexuality, and prostitution as vehicles of patriarchal society and believe that all these institutions must be abolished (Willis, 1984). Some radical feminists support separatism, the limiting of relationships with men as a means to achieve change. Unlike liberal feminists, who support political action to change the status of women, radical feminists believe that in order for women to be freed from oppression, societal and cultural structures that support the patriarchy must be eliminated (Willis, 1984).

According to Smith and Smith (1983), "Feminism is the political theory and practice to free all women: women of color, working-class women, poor women, physically challenged women, lesbians, old women, as well as white economically privileged heterosexual women. Anything less than this is not feminism, but merely female self-aggrandizement" (p. 121). All people interested in a progressive agenda must work to end all oppression at the intersections and at the margins. The view of race, gender, and class as intersecting social concerns has important implications for change (Dawson, 2001).

Sexual Orientation

Sexual orientation is complex in history, context, and embodiment. Although the term "homosexual" did not exist until 1869, lesbians, gays, and bisexuals have existed across time and cultures (Tully, 2000). Bisexuality was unrecognized and therefore invisible until very recently (Boston Women's Health Book Collective, 1998; Garnets & Peplau, 2001). In some contexts, differing sexual orientations have been condemned; in others, they have been normalized and sometimes even exalted (Tully). Most Native American cultures view sexuality as well as gender beyond the dichotomy used by many others in the United States (Tafoya, 1997).

Lesbian, gay, and bisexual individuals from communities of color may experience oppression in the community at large as well as in their ethnic community (Garnets & Peplau, 2001). They may also experience racism in gay, lesbian, and bisexual communities. Lesbian, gay, and bisexual individuals of color are frequently marginalized and made invisible. As we work in a multicultural context to dismantle oppression, we often overlook the nexus of racism and heterosexism (Kumashiro, 2001). However, more and more, the voices of gay, lesbian, and bisexual individuals of color have been surfacing (Hidalgo, 1995). For example, Garrett (2001) and Romo-Carmona (1995) explore individual and collective stories of lesbian Latinas, and Chan (2001) and Bruining (1995a, 1995b) tell stories of Asian American lesbians.

Sexual orientation is flexible and multifaceted (Garnets, 2002). Knowing whether a person is heterosexual, homosexual, or bisexual tells us little when we are not aware of the whole context. It tells us nothing about the quality of her or his life. It does not tell us about aspects of her or his life such as relationships, values and ethics, family, children or grandchildren, housing, employment, or politics.

Increasing political awareness of LGB people and issues has given rise to demands for recognition, acceptance, and rights. While lesbian and gay people have always formed partnerships, joined families, and raised children, they are now increasingly demanding legal recognition of their relationships and families. The move to legitimize gay marriage is making headway. As of this writing (readers are encouraged to check for the most current information), marriages between same-sex couples are legal in Canada, Belgium, Spain, South Africa, and the Netherlands. Other countries (such as New Zealand and Switzerland) have adopted civil union laws that confer the same rights as marriage to both heterosexual and same-sex couples, and some—such as Mexico, France, Portugal, and Denmark—have implemented laws that bestow some but not all of the rights of marriage to same-sex couples (these frequently do not grant rights related to adoption or immigration). In the United States, only Massachusetts performs marriages between individuals of the same sex, while the unions of same-sex couples are recognized in Vermont, Connecticut, California, Hawaii, New Jersey, Maine, New Hampshire, Oregon, and Washington, DC, through civil unions, domestic partner laws, and reciprocal benefits. The courts in Massachusetts and Iowa ruled that denial of the right of marriage to lesbians and gay men violates the state constitution, although Iowa still does not permit same-sex marriage. The move to legitimize gay unions has gained momentum in several other states as well. Unfortunately, the backlash in response to this change is gaining momentum as well.

Discrimination against people who are lesbian, gay, and bisexual in the United States occurs in both personal relationships and societal structures (Herek, 1998). LGB people live with the daily experience and impact of homophobia (Pharr, 2000; Taylor, 2002). They also experience the effects of heterosexism, according to which heterosexuality is superior to homosexuality and bisexuality. Heterosexism in the United States centers heterosexual behavior as normal and stigmatizes homosexual and bisexual behavior; this is reinforced through institutionalized prejudice and discrimination (Garnets, 2002; Herek, 1998). Because "heterosexuality is taken for granted" (Moi, 1999, p. 12), gay, lesbian, and bisexual people suffer the oppression of invisibility and secrecy.

The assumption that marriage should be between a man and a woman is one example of heterosexism. Homophobia makes many lesbian, gay, and bisexual individuals fearful that they will lose friends, family, their employment, and their housing if they are honest about their sexual orientation. A life lived in secrecy out of fear of reprisal takes an emotional toll. Even worse are the consequences of homophobia that can lead to the loss of children; to abuse; and to suicide, the risk of which is high for gay, lesbian, and bisexual youths (Pharr, 2000).

There is ongoing resistance to efforts to address homophobia and alleviate the oppression of lesbians, gay men, and bisexuals. "Homophobia is usually the last oppression to be mentioned, the last to be taken seriously, the last to go. But it is extremely serious, sometimes to the point of being fatal" (Smith, 1983, p. 7). One reason is the fear many people have that others will conclude that they are not heterosexual; another reason is that neglecting the subject of homophobia allows heterosexuals to maintain their privilege (Smith, 1983). Although homosexuality has not been viewed by the American Psychological Association as a mental illness since 1973, social work practice based on bias, lack of knowledge, and inadequate services is still prevalent (Hancock, 2000). Yet those committed to social and economic justice have a responsibility to dismantle all forms of oppression, including homophobia (Lorde, 1983; National Association of Social Workers, 2001).

Homophobia is used to enforce sexism by keeping women and men in rigid sex roles. The fear that many people have of being labeled lesbian or gay, along with the concomitant discrimination, hatred, and violence fuelled by homophobia, works to keep women's and men's behavior within the confines of that deemed acceptable by traditional gender role expectations. According to Pharr (1993), political attacks by conservatives on lesbians and gay men divert "people from grasping their overall agenda of dismantling the gains of the Civil Rights Movement and democracy itself" (p. 1). Conservatives and religious fundamentalists denigrate homosexuality and bisexuality and instill fear by persuading their constituents that lesbian, gay, and bisexual people are a threat to their marriages and way of life.

The groups that oppose feminism and the Equal Rights Amendment are often the same groups that speak out against lesbians and gay men (Faludi, 1991; Pharr, 1993, 2000). The current controversy raging around same-sex marriage is an example of how most conservative religious organizations promote rigid gender roles.

Joining the Web of Oppression

The concepts of gender and sexual orientation, like race and ethnicity, are unstable. They are complex and, like race, have different meanings to different people. While the history and manifestation of discrimination of people of color differ from that of lesbians and gay men, people in these groups share the experience of navigating institutionalized oppression (Greene, 2000). Most analyses of race, class, religion, gender, ethnicity, ability, and age are silent on the subject of sexual orientation, which creates the assumption that all people in these groups are heterosexual (Greene, 2000). The assumption that all lesbians and gay men are white and affluent denies the complexity of their lives and communities.

Women, people who are transgender, and people who are lesbian, gay, and bisexual fit Young's criteria for an oppressed group. They experience all five faces of oppression: exploitation, marginalization, powerlessness, cultural imperialism, and violence. In addition, the oppression of women interlocks with oppressions based on racism, classism, and homophobia. Women of color, along with lesbian and bisexual women, are exposed to double jeopardy. Lesbians of color experience triple jeopardy.

The theoretical perspective of critical multiculturalism makes the point that none of the categories in the multicultural spectrum stands alone. We cannot talk about gender, sex, and sexual orientation without talking about race, ethnicity, and class. They are all part of the web of oppression. From this perspective, the study of gender is incomplete without an examination of the varied social locations and experiences of women. The interlocking systems of oppression, which affect individuals differently based on gender, sex, sexual orientation, race, ethnicity, national origin, and class, "affect access to power and privileges, influence social relationships, construct meanings and shape people's everyday experience" (Ngan-ling, 1996, p. xix).

Chapter 5

People with Disabilities

> Just as the dominant culture's ideal self requires the ideological figures of the woman to confirm its masculinity and of the black to assure its whiteness, so Emerson's atomized self demands an oppositional twin to secure its able-bodiness.
>
> R. J. Thomson, *Extraordinary Bodies*

Our families and communities are vulnerable to disabilities. As one in five adults have a disability, most of us are affected personally or have friends, family members, or coworkers who experience a disability. As a result of injury, disease, and simple aging, each of us can become disabled (Stroman, 2003). The impact can be devastating. For some, however, disability offers an opportunity to build resilience, as many individuals and families find great strength in surmounting obstacles (see box 5.1).

Box 5.1   *Disability and Resilience*

My disability doesn't define me, though it certainly did change my life. As a white male, I had privileges. Developing some empathy through reflection on my childhood difficulties and then choosing to work with very strong women gave me some awareness of my privilege. I did my best to use that privilege to empower others. Little did I know that I would have a chance to get to intimately know the impact of oppression and struggle.

Not long after becoming a single parent, I was diagnosed with multiple sclerosis. The loss of my wife, my expanded parenting role, and my illness led me to leave a stressful work environment. My whole self-concept changed. I now had the role of a full-time parent; I no longer had a professional role. My multiple sclerosis progressed quickly. My role as a parent has been and continues to be a wonderful part of my life.

Sometimes I have been angry. The unfairness periodically grips my emotions. Mostly, I feel blessed to have had the opportunity to raise spectacular children. Through hardship, I have come to understand myself better, and my children have had the opportunity to develop into competent, compassionate, caring adults.

Some disabilities are visible; others are not. Some are present at birth; others are not. While some progress slowly, others strike suddenly. It can happen in seconds with an accident or a medical crisis. It can build over time, possibly resulting from or in a major medical or psychiatric illness. It might result in an inability to work for long periods of time. The loss of income and change in socioeconomic status that can result are disruptive and life changing. The risk of disability increases with age. The elderly are four times more likely to live with a disability. Individuals over eighty-five years of age are five times more likely to experience disability than those between sixty-five and sixty-nine years of age (Guralnik & Simonsick, 1993).

Some people have physical differences, which are not disabilities but nonetheless can create barriers to relationships. While physical differences such as anatomical anomalies, scars, and disfigurements may not constitute a disability, they can create a social disability: "What causes disability, then, is the reaction of others—the horror, the fascination, the fear, the pity, all reactions that erode self-esteem and can easily cause the avoidance of public spaces and public events" (Rothman, 2003, p. 146).

Disabilities can also strike children and have a profound impact on the individual and the family. Overall, 8 percent of children experience a disability. The rate increases with age, and boys are almost twice as likely as girls to experience a disability. Cerebral palsy, spina bifida, orthopedic disabilities, muscular dystrophy, and visual and hearing impairments are the disabilities that are common among children (Jivanjee, 1999). Children can also experience developmental, learning, and mental disabilities. These can result in functional limitations such as learning difficulties, emotional obstacles, developmental delays, and mental retardation. Other illnesses such as asthma, congenital heart disease, and seizure disorders can result in disabilities that severely impair children's ability to participate in many daily activities.

Demographics

While it is difficult to quantify the number of people living with some form of disability, it is a fact that the number is substantial (United Nations, 2006). From a global perspective, approximately one-tenth of the population (more than half a billion people) live with a disability (Priestly, 2001). Of these, 80 percent live in developing countries (United Nations, 2006).

In the United States, approximately 18 percent of the population (51 million individuals) live with some type of disability; almost a third (10 million) require assistance with activities of daily living (U.S. Census Bureau, 2006b). More than 63 percent of people with disabilities (32 million) are considered to have a severe disability (U.S. Census Bureau, 2006b).

Disabilities experienced by children vary by age and gender. While only 3 percent of children under six have a disability, the rate is almost four times higher for children between the ages of six and fourteen years old (U.S. Census Bureau, 2006b). Most (92%) children under the age of six with disabilities experience developmental disabilities; 31 percent have mobility difficulties. Sixty-three percent of children up to the age of fourteen with a disability are male. The vast majority (78%) of disabilities for children age six to fourteen are learning or developmental disabilities. Eighteen percent experience mobility issues and 18 percent have speech disabilities, while 5 percent have hearing difficulties, and another 5 percent have vision limitations (U.S. Census Bureau, 2006b).

Overall, women have higher rates of disabilities (19.5%) than men (16.7%), and they make up the majority (55%) of people with disabilities. However, this varies based on age and race/ethnicity. While the rate of disability is lower for females than males from childhood to the age of twenty-five, the trend reverses for adults age twenty-five years and older (Steinmetz, 2006). This is true of all ethnic groups, except Latinos/Latinas between fifteen and twenty-four, among whom 8.5 percent of both males and females have disabilities (Steinmetz, 2006). Among adults age sixty-five and older, 40.5 percent of women have a severe disability, compared to 31.9 percent of men (U.S. Census Bureau, 2006b). Sadly, it is estimated that between 33 and 83 percent of women with disabilities have been victims of physical or sexual abuse (Schaller & Lagergren Frieberg, 1998).

The likelihood that a person will have a severe disability varies by race and ethnicity. Across age groups, the prevalence rates for disabilities and severe disabilities among African Americans are higher than for any other race. Overall, severe disabilities occur at a rate of 14 percent for African Americans, 11.8 percent for non-Latino whites, 8.8 percent for Latinos, and 7.2 percent for Asians and Pacific Islanders (Steinmetz, 2006). In general, these rates remain consistent across age; African Americans maintain the highest rate of severe disabilities compared to all other ethnicities by age, and Asians have the lowest rates of disabilities compared to all ethnicities by age except among those age sixty-five and older. The rate of severe disabilities for Latinos over age sixty-five is the lowest (32.8%). It is 35.2 percent for non-Latino whites, 36.9 percent for Asians and Pacific Islanders, and 49.5 percent for blacks. Of people with disabilities who are receiving Social Security Disability Insurance, 70 percent are white, and 17 percent are black (U.S. General Accounting Office, 2003).

Poverty, family structure, age, and disability also interact. Almost twice as many children with disabilities live in single-parent families as in two-parent families. Families in which at least one person has a disability experience higher poverty rates (12.8%) than other families (7.7%). The rate of poverty for children with disabilities is 29 percent, compared to 17 percent for children without disabilities (U.S. Census Bureau, 2005a). The poverty rate continues to be higher for people with disabilities than for people without disabilities, across age groups. Poverty rates for people between twenty-five and sixty-four years of age are higher for people with disabilities. The poverty rate is 2.6 times higher when the disability is not severe, and 3.4 times higher for people with severe disabilities. While the poverty rate for people without disabilities is 8.3, it is 27.9 for people with severe disabilities (Rothman, 2003).

Defining Disability

Culture plays a role in the definition, interpretation, and evaluation of disabilities. The meanings attached to disability differ among cultures and over time. Language and context frame people's perceptions and actions. The English language abounds with negative expressions related to disability (Linton, 1998; Snyder, Brueggemann, & Thomson, 2002). There are many expressions regarding health and a sound body, such as "If you don't have your health, you have nothing," "What, are you blind?" and "What, are you deaf?" (Michalko, 2002, p. 43).

There are both individual and social models for framing disability issues (see Rothman, 2003, for a thorough discussion). The individual models (such as the moral, deficit, social Darwinist, eugenics, and medical models) locate the problem within the person with a disability. The social models (oppression, diversity, and social construction models) locate the problem within the context of the environment, social structures, values, and supports.

The medical model builds from the deficit model. Too often, the medical profession focuses on labeling and diagnosing. The person with a disability is conceptualized as failing to meet the normal standards of ability, mobility, and how the human body should be. The individual body is considered at fault and treated with medical interventions. Disability is treated as a continuous struggle toward normalcy. People with disabilities are seen as abnormal, weak, and helpless (Zola, 1993). The medical model was the dominant paradigm for many years and continues to frame some belief systems and patterns of thinking.

The paradigm shift to social models moved the location of the problem from the individual to society (Michalko, 2002). This shift recasts the individual's limitations as the product of society's failure to provide appropriate services (Michalko, 2002). These models acknowledge the restrictions imposed by institutional discrimination, inaccessible spaces, and inadequate support systems and recognizes the oppressive nature of negative social views, which stereotype and lead to the isolation of disabled individuals and make them invisible (Oliver, 1996; Rothman, 2003). Social models pay attention to the potential for these attitudes to result in the internalization of negative images of disability among people with disabilities.

There is no clear consensus on the definition of disability. Multiple social science, legal, and policy definitions have developed. The U.S. Census Bureau (2006b) defines disability as "a reduced ability to perform tasks one would normally do at a given stage in life." The U.S. Department of Justice's (2005) definition targets the individual, focusing on physical and mental impairments that limit life activities. The ambiguity and multiplicity of definitions leave room for political or moral judgment based on societal attitudes about and perceptions of disability (Kudlick, 2003).

Some definitions are used as eligibility criteria for services. Legal and policy definitions underlie the implementation of Social Security Disability Insurance (SSDI), Supplemental Security Income (SSI), and the Americans with Disabilities Act (ADA). The definitions used by SSDI and SSI are based on the individual model, in which disabilities are viewed as a loss that may require compensation. Under the ADA, a disability is defined as physical or mental impairment that limits one or more life activities and is regarded by society as an impairment; to qualify, an individual must be able to provide documentation of the impairment (U.S. Department of Justice, 2005). This definition is multileveled, leaving room for interpretation.

Two primary disability programs that pay benefits, SSDI and SSI, rely on the definition of disability in the Social Security Act. This definition is based on the medical model. To be eligible, an individual has to have been unable to engage in employment as a result of a physical or mental disability for at least twelve months. In addition to having a disability, to be eligible for SSDI, an individual has to have worked and contributed to the Social Security insurance program; for SSI, which is means tested, applicants must meet income and asset guidelines. More than 161 million Americans are covered by Social Security Disability Insurance. About 6.5 million disabled workers (and their 1.8 million dependents) receive Social Security Disability Insurance benefits (Social Security Administration, 2007). More than a third (36%) of the people receiving SSDI benefits are people with a mental disorder. This amounts to approximately $90 billion in federal spending, or nearly 5 percent of the federal budget (Stroman, 2003).

The social paradigm formed the thinking behind the ADA. Unlike programs based on the individual medical model, the ADA focuses on safeguarding the rights of people who are disabled. People with disabilities were not guaranteed that public spaces would be accessible for them until the passage of this act (Thomson, 1997). The ADA moved policy from one of compensation to one of accommodation. Job discrimination against an individual with a disability who is able to function on the job with (or without) reasonable accommodations is prohibited. Discrimination against workers who have impairments but who are nonetheless able to perform the essential functions of the jobs they seek to hold or retain is banned. Employers are now required by law to make reasonable accommodations for employees.

Children and Families

Families of children with disabilities experience multiple strains and hardships (Jivanjee, 1999). Children and families encounter social stigma, physical barriers, and deficit-based medical and human service systems. In addition, families of children with disabilities frequently have to struggle with school systems to get adequate accommodations for their children. Attending to the care and advocacy needs of children with disabilities can be draining and requires a great amount of time.

Response systems have changed over time. Children who were deaf or blind used to be placed in segregated schools. Now, with the changes in technology and new policies, they are frequently integrated into regular classrooms. New policies and laws require school systems to provide accommodations for students. There has been movement away from viewing the problem as a personal one and toward defining the problem as structural and systemic. Too often, however, systems slip back into the deficit model, which blames the individual and family and requires families to invest intensively in advocating for accommodations. The case in box 5.2 provides an example of a family struggling to decide on a course of action to take for a child with a hearing disability.

Box 5.2   *My Son Is Deaf*

I remember the day in July when I finally received the diagnosis. I had started to suspect that my son was deaf a few days after his adoption in Vietnam. He was five months old, and we were with a group of other children the same age who were also being adopted. There was a very loud bang, and all the children jumped except Michael. After that moment, I took notice of his response to other noises. There was none. For the most part, I kept my suspicions to myself, as I did not want other people in the group to view me as a hypochondriac. I did, however, tell my partner about my suspicions. She downplayed my concerns and took every opportunity to show me when he was engaged and seemed to respond to a sound.

Once we were home, we worked on getting Michael checked for various possible medical conditions that are common among internationally adopted children, as well as some respiratory concerns that needed to be addressed. On one of the many visits to the pediatrician's office, I mentioned my concern to him. He also downplayed my concerns, stating that it could be due to the fluid that Michael seemed to have in his ears. However, our pediatrician agreed to have him evaluated at Children's Hospital. Unfortunately though, Michael could not be sedated for the test until his respiratory issues were resolved.

As we settled in and I started to become more and more concerned, I began to mention my concerns to family members and friends. They would say that they felt that Michael was fine and would point out all the times that he responded to people. The turning point occurred when the car alarm went off while Michael was in the car. Although the rest of us jumped, Michael did not wake up. Even then, my family still insisted that he was not having problems hearing. I recall returning home one day after my parents had watched Michael for the day. Apparently, they took the opportunity to test his hearing. They blew a whistle close to his ears and banged pots and pans to see if he would respond. At times he did. I suspect that at those times he was responding to their movement. At other times, he did not respond. After their test, my mother started to realize that Michael had some hearing problems. My father was still in denial.

On the day that Michael did not pass the ABR test, we were immediately thrown into the whirlwind of decision making and appointments. We left the hospital with a packet of information about the communications department at Children's Hospital and communication options, and an appointment for a loaner hearing aid. We were also instructed to apply for Medicaid to help with the cost of hearing aids and the other related medical costs of being deaf. We were not given time to grieve the loss of the perfectly healthy, hearing child for whom we had planned. The professionals mistakenly felt that since we had had a strong suspicion of our son's hearing impairment and because he was adopted, we would not need the same time to grieve as other couples who are the biological parents of children with a similar diagnosis. I had preconceived ideas about what it means to be deaf. Many of these ideas had to do with what I perceived to be the limitations of what deaf people are able to do and what I perceived to be the isolation of the deaf community. This was not what I wanted for my beautiful infant son.

As I began to tell people of Michael's diagnosis, everyone had an opinion of what would be the best method of communication for Michael. "He should learn American Sign Language." "He should learn to cue." "He should be in a total communication program." "He should learn to listen and speak." Every professional felt free to express her or his opinion. I quickly ruled out cueing, as the number of people who can cue is limited. The decision between ASL, auditory verbal communication, and total communication was much more difficult. I struggled with whether to have him learn ASL. This would give him a community and culture of which he could be a part. From my experience, the deaf community appears to be a close community with a history and culture of its own. He would have the support of a community to help him develop a sense of self as a deaf person. However, choosing ASL as his primary mode of communicating would isolate him from most of his family, all of whom are able to hear, and the hearing community in general. I also wondered how it would limit his career opportunities and how he would manage with simple things like ordering food in a restaurant. If I chose to have him in an auditory-verbal program and he learned to listen and speak, it would give him access to the hearing world, increase his future career opportunities, and make it easier for him to develop relationships with his extended family. But would he always feel like an outsider, different from hearing people? Could he become comfortable with his deafness in a hearing world? In some ways, total communication looked like a compromise between ASL and auditory verbal communication. I soon realized that total communication programs tend to favor one or the other approach. I wondered if he could truly become English-ASL bilingual. Would total communication provide him with the communication skills necessary to maximize his overall learning? My head was spinning as I contemplated this decision that would have a major impact on my son's life.

> Really what I needed at the time was someone who would listen to my concerns, educate me about the differences, and help me look at the pros and cons of each choice. It would have been helpful to have been connected to other parents of children who were hearing impaired. Friends and family expressed their sympathy and then did everything they could to avoid talking about Michael's deafness. Perhaps part of it was my discomfort with talking about it also. I was feeling alone in my grief with very few supports.

Parents of children who acquire a disability embark on a painful journey from life as it existed before to a different life with a child who has a changed future and a transformed daily existence (Cohen Konrad, 2003). This is true whether the disability results from a sudden injury or a slow progression through illness. The unanticipated change caused by the disability and the sense of loss can be painful. It is, however, a process that can create a transformation in the parent as well as the child (Cohen Konrad, 2003).

Types of Disabilities

Disabilities are generally divided into four categories: sensory (e.g., deafness, hearing impairments, blindness, visual impairments); physical (e.g., spinal cord injury, diabetes, acquired brain injury, multiple sclerosis, scoliosis, cerebral palsy, arthritis, amputation, short stature); mental (e.g., developmental disabilities, mental illness, dementia); and intellectual/learning disabilities.

When people think and talk about disabilities, most often it is physical disabilities and issues of mobility that come to mind (Rothman, 2003). Conditions within the environment create barriers that reinforce institutional discrimination (Barnes, 1991). These barriers can take many forms, including broken roads and sidewalk surfaces and ineffective mobility aids, as well as a lack of educational, visual, and auditory supports. Those who are visibly disabled, whether physically or mentally, draw unwanted attention and have historically been regarded as "sick, suffering, diseased and in pain" (Barnes & Mercer, 2003, p. 10).

Sensory Disabilities

In the United States, people defined as disabled include almost 8 million people with vision impairments, over 7 million with hearing impairments, and over 2 million with speech impairments (Steinmetz, 2006). The percentage of people with hearing loss increases with age, reaching over 70 percent by eighty-five years of age (Weinstein, 2002). Blindness, deafness, and other forms of visual and hearing impairments can be present from birth or develop later as a result of illness or injury. Blindness as well as deafness is often understood in terms of the medical model. Because the able-bodied place a high value on sight and hearing, blindness and deafness are viewed as a catastrophe.

Among the deaf and hard of hearing there are distinctions based on the amount and timing of hearing loss. Those who were born deaf or lost their hearing early in life are more likely to participate in the deaf culture (Luey, Glass, & Elliott, 1995). Deaf communities are tightly knit with clear boundaries and high rates of marriage within the community. "More than any other group with disabilities, deaf people have developed a distinct and separate culture within the wider U.S. cultural mosaic. Deaf culture has all of the distinguishing marks of a culture: a language, terminology and expressions, criteria for participation and membership, and an established way of interacting, as a culture, with other cultures" (Rothman, 2003, p. 135).

Mental Disabilities

Mental disabilities range broadly, and people with mental disabilities are a vulnerable population. Included are people with developmental disabilities, mental illness, Alzheimer's, and dementia. Education and training of people with mental disabilities, their families, and the community at large can foster the development of increased potential for independence and productivity.

Mental illness is a form of disability that, when visible, can result in extreme stigma. Mental illness is often judged negatively by society and affects the individuals who suffer from mental illness as well as their family, friends, and communities. Mental illnesses are socially constructed, with definitions that vary by culture and shift over time. Behavior that is acceptable in one culture may not be in another. The ADA requires accommodations for individuals with mental illness, but these can be poorly implemented and mental health systems may be stressed by the cyclical nature of some illnesses (Rothman, 2003).

Learning/Cognitive Disabilities

Learning and cognitive disabilities, speech impairments, and attention-deficit/hyperactivity disorder affect families and educational and work environments. Without accommodations, these disabilities, though often not readily apparent to the casual observer, can affect a person's ability to learn. Learning disabilities can interfere with listening, speaking, writing, reading, reasoning, and social skills (Rothman, 2003).

Physical Disabilities

For people with visible physical disabilities, "the disability itself becomes one of the factors in the interaction [with non-disabled persons], often determining the quality and quantity of relationships" (Rothman, 2003, p. 144). For those experiencing disabilities that are not immediately visible to others, decisions must be made regarding when to disclose the disability, and when not to disclose. Some pivotal and frequently stressful places where these decisions must be made are school, work, and relationships.

People with visible physical disabilities too often experience the oppression of unwanted attention. Others' stares are an example of the power relations between the subject position of people with disabilities and the able-bodied (Thomson, 2001). The staring dynamic establishes the starer as normal and the object of the stares as different.

Historically, society's focus on perfection and beauty has resulted in the absence of images of people with disabilities in the media (Hahn, 1987). Seldom are people with disabilities "portrayed as ordinary people doing ordinary things and, consequently, they are viewed as 'other'" (Northway, 1997, p. 738). Contributing to the invisibility of people with visible disabilities is others' avoidance of those with disabilities, which results from people's fear of becoming disabled. Although representations of people with visible disabilities are still not common in the media, since the passage of the ADA in 1990, advertisers have become aware of this market. As a result, the number of advertisements, television shows, and movies featuring characters with disabilities has increased, although these are still generally attractive people with non-disfiguring disabilities. For example, the movies *The Horse Whisperer* (1998) and *I Am Sam* (2001) focus on characters with disabilities, and people in wheelchairs have appeared in television and print advertisements for companies such as McDonald's, Nike, Levi's, and Target. There is a significant market among people with disabilities over the age of fifteen, who have an estimated income of $700 billion with discretionary funds (Bauman, 2005).

History

Classical thinkers such as Aristotle established the definition of the perfect human body. People whose bodies did not meet the ideals of the perfect human body were described as deformed or deviant (Garland, 1995). Aristotle and Plato suggested that parents should not raise infants or children with disabilities but should abandon or kill them instead, and early Roman law admonished parents to kill children with disabilities.

The Judeo-Christian values, philosophy, and traditions of Europe have affected the views and treatment of people with disabilities in the United States (Appleby, Colon, & Hamilton, 2001). The Elizabethan poor laws of England isolated people with disabilities in almshouses. During the Enlightenment, disabilities began to be seen as a matter of biological inadequacies. It was at this point that people with visible disabilities became identified with their disabilities. Social Darwinism (in the late 1800s to mid-1900s) supported the perception that people with disabilities are weak and inferior and that reproduction by people with disabilities hurts the human race. The response was primarily one of stigma, isolation, and charity. During the nineteenth century, the moral model, according to which people with disabilities were being punished for something they had done wrong, prevailed (Rothman, 2003). Proponents of these beliefs provided charity to people with disabilities, although recipients had no right to expect anything and therefore needed to be grateful for whatever they received.

The so-called ugly laws of the nineteenth century placed social restrictions on people with an offensive or frightening physical appearance (Barnes & Mercer, 2003; Bryan, 1999). During this same time period, the circus provided a space for the display of people with visible disabilities for the amusement and profit of others (Bogdan, 1988). These so-called freak shows flourished in Europe and North America from the mid-1800s to the mid-1900s.

From colonial times to the present, U.S. immigration laws have at different times banned immigration by people with certain disabilities. For example, in 1896 immigrants who were "deaf, dumb, blind, idiotic, insane, pauper, and criminal" were not allowed to immigrate (Baynton, 2001, p. 47). In 1917, the list of disabilities on the basis of which immigration could be denied grew to include ailments such as asthma, arthritis, flat feet, and varicose veins. A 1949 court ruling (*United States v. Schwarz*) ruled that immigrants with mental illness could be refused entrance to the United States, and in 1993, at the request of the National Institute of Health, the United States passed legislation prohibiting people living with HIV or AIDS from immigrating, and non–U.S. citizens with HIV or AIDS from entering the country for travel. This law remains in effect.

The social isolation and institutionalization of people with disabilities continued until the 1960s. Up to this time, individuals with disabilities were seen as shameful, the source of disgrace (Appleby et al., 2001). Throughout history, people with visible disabilities have been viewed as a family burden and have been hidden in attics. This began to change in the early twentieth century with the shift toward the medical model and the building of large psychiatric institutions (Rothman, 2003). It was during the last part of the twentieth century that the idea of disability as a social construct emerged (see Stiker, 1999, for a thorough discussion).

A more aware and humane social consciousness only began to emerge after World Wars I and II (Appleby et al., 2001). After World War I, large numbers of veterans returned home with injuries. The government provided veterans, who were seen as the worthy disabled, with rehabilitation services (Rothman, 2003). The Vocational Rehabilitation Act of 1920 was the first piece of federal legislation to address the issues of disabled veterans (Appleby et al., 2001). Most other people with disabilities still did not have access to resources (Rothman, 2003). World War II slowed the progress toward a more humane treatment of people with disabilities. With the end of the war, however, new federal legislation was introduced that was responding to both the needs of the returning veterans as well as the horrors of the war, during which the Nazis exterminated 250,000 people with disabilities and subjected even more to experiments (Rothman, 2003).

The last half of the twentieth century witnessed the closing of mental health institutions and the empowerment of individuals with disabilities (Rothman, 2003). The 1970s marked the beginning of the disabilities movement with the emergence of organized political action and cultural movements. Disabilities rights organizations, which formed during the 1970s and 1980s, advocated legislation that steered society from seeing disability as an individual responsibility to viewing it as a social responsibility (see Rothman, 2003, for a full history). Throughout the last several decades, the disabilities movement has made progress in breaking down barriers, altering worldviews, and passing rights legislation (Appleby et al., 2001). The ADA, the most comprehensive rights legislation addressing the needs of people with disabilities, passed in 1990. This legislation calls "for the elimination of all forms of discrimination through the development of enforceable standards and clarifies the role of the federal government in overseeing enforcement of the provisions of the act" (Rothman, 2003, p. 48). People with disabilities have entered the mainstream.

Oppression of People with Disabilities

People with disabilities are recognized as an oppressed group (Oliver, 1996). Their oppression, like that experienced by other oppressed groups, is both active and passive, resulting from structural factors and also from "the fact that this structure is not questioned" (Northway, 1997, p. 738). Historically, the concept of disability has been used to marginalize women, African Americans, and immigrants of color by supporting the claim that they are unfit for full citizenship (Kudlick, 2003). This has resulted in unfavorable policy decisions for all these groups.

Young's five faces of oppression (exploitation, marginalization, powerlessness, cultural imperialism, and violence) can be applied to the oppression experienced by people with disabilities. The oppression to which people with disabilities are subjected may be compounded by other forms of oppression. In a system of overlapping oppressions, women with identifiable disabilities, like women of color, have been marginalized economically, socially, and politically. There are parallels between the value assigned to female bodies and those attributed to disabled bodies (Thomson, 1997). The bodies of people who are physically challenged, as well as those of women and people of color, have been labeled by society as inferior and deviant.

The dehumanization of people with disabilities leads to physical violence and social isolation. People who are visibly physically or mentally disabled experience a high rate of overt and covert violence. This violence is related to cultural imperialism. Cultural imperialism, which establishes able-bodiedness as the cultural norm, creates an environment in which people with disabilities are exploited and marginalized (Michalko, 2002; Thomson, 1997). When measured against the norm, difference is seen as less than (Northway, 1997). As a result of ableism, the defining of people with disabilities in a negative and stereotypical manner, individuals with disabilities are perceived as deficient or deviant, and it is generally expected that they will not have fulfilling roles in life (Mackelprang & Salsgiver, 1999).

Able-bodiedness is seen as natural; if one is not able-bodied, then one is different or defective and therefore the "other." The viewing of people with visible disabilities as less than human results in differential treatment (Northway, 1997). This negative view is often internalized by people with disabilities. While the assumptions about people with less visible disabilities may not be as negative as those held about people with more visible disabilities, they can nonetheless affect daily living and the long-range opportunities of people with disabilities. For example, skeptical educational personnel may fail to provide appropriate accommodations and resources for those with learning disabilities.

The marginalization of people with disabilities is further enabled by poorly supported education, inadequate and exploitative employment, social stigma, misdirected health policy, and limited political resources. The physical environment serves to maintain marginalization. "Disabled people are often placed in a situation in which they are expected to conform to the expectations of others, to take orders but seldom to give them" (Northway, 1997, p. 739). Many people believe that persons with disabilities don't have the power to determine their own needs or achieve their goals. Disabled individuals are underrepresented in the professions and management; conversely, they are overrepresented in low-skilled, poorly paid, and less secure positions (Roulsone, 1998). People with disabilities are too often sidelined in the labor force; they experience high rates of unemployment and have difficulty finding employment. This results not only from perceived limitations, but also from an education that marginalized them and failed to meet their needs.

Despite the efforts of the ADA and the disabilities movement, disability is often constructed as a physical inadequacy, a catastrophe for which people must be pitied and compensated. The "otherness" of people who are disabled has been exploited as a source of entertainment and for fund-raising efforts (Barnes & Mercer, 2003). Images of people with disability are used in advertising and soliciting campaigns by charity organizations (for example, in telethons) and helping societies (such as the Easter Seals). "Even when intentions are altruistic, fund-raisers such as telethons have repeatedly created pity and exploited guilt to achieve their purposes" (Mackelprang & Salsgiver, 1999, p. 5). One of the consequences of the exploitive use of these images is the reinforcement of negative stereotypes. Feminist disability studies, which challenge assumptions and unsettle stereotypes regarding disability, focus on rights and the redressing of exclusion from society (Thomson, 2005). In this process, voices that speak up for rights and against discrimination are no longer silenced.

Joining the Web of Oppression

Over the past twenty years there have been numerous articles and monographs on the subject of disability. The fields that took up the challenge of studying race, gender, and sexuality have provided valuable analytic and theoretical tools for exploring this "other" that has often been left out of anti-oppression analysis

(Kudlick, 2003). Recent works on disability studies move from using an individual medical pathology to defining disability as a social category on par with race, class, and gender (Linton, 1998; Potok, 2002).

Wilson and Lewieki-Wilson (2001) assert that "one's social location and identity within a given society in terms of race, class, and gender affect what it means to be disabled" (p. 10). Women, in relationship to the male "norm," are seen as being unequal because of their supposed physical, intellectual, and psychological flaws. In comparison to men, women are viewed as physically weak and excessively emotional (Baynton, 2001). In the mid-nineteenth century, people of color were routinely associated with people with disabilities. Slavery was often justified by the supposition that African Americans lacked sufficient intelligence to participate in society on an equal basis. Another example is the naming of individuals with Down syndrome as Mongoloid in 1866. John Langdon Down, who worked at an institution for children with developmental disabilities, noticed physical similarities among one group of the children, whom he labeled Mongoloids because he thought they looked like people from Mongolia (who were thought to be intellectually inferior) (Tarek, 2005). The naming of this syndrome denigrated both the race and the disability.

Historically, the concept of disability has been used to view different groups of people as disabled and justify their unequal treatment, just as sexist and racist beliefs and misconceptions have been used to justify discrimination against women and people of color (Baynton, 2001). Unfortunately, people with disabilities are subjected to discrimination within other rights movements. A variety of mechanisms, including isolation and the use of negative terminology, enforce their marginalization.

People with disabilities can experience multiple overlapping oppressions. People with disabilities can experience oppression arising from class, gender, age, and sexual orientation and the various intersecting oppressions that result. For example, for people who were not born with disabilities but become disabled as a result of illness or injury, the shift from privilege to the oppression of disability can bring with it the oppression of economic hardship. It can be difficult to adjust to the isolation and stigmatization of disability. For some, this difficulty provides an opportunity to understand the oppression of others.

The isolation that people with disabilities experience is often denied because no one wants to admit avoiding them or wishing them harm. Some marginalized groups have had success campaigning for a more positive public image; disability, however, is still associated with negative stereotypes. Approaching disability as a social category rather than as an individual attribute allows society to move the discussion and responsibility for change into a more open arena and allows the public to see it not just as a matter of interest to people in rehabilitation, special education, and related fields (Kudlick, 2003). Communities and organizations have the opportunity and obligation to provide the resources necessary for everyone, including those living with disabilities, to reach their potential.

Chapter 6

Creating Your Web: Positioning and Shifting

> It is not difference which immobilizes us, but silence. And there are so many silences to be broken.
>
> Audre Lorde, *Sister Outsider: Essays and Speeches*

The previous chapters laid the groundwork for the exploration of historically oppressed groups and communities, and the integration and synthesis of that information in this chapter. Critical multiculturalism and Young's five faces of oppression provided the theoretical framework for examination and evaluation. Self-reflection integrated with historical, political, and developmental knowledge building followed. Race and ethnicity; gender, sex, and sexual orientation; and ability status were examined through the theoretical lens of critical multiculturalism.

Critical multiculturalism is a multidimensional, multifaceted, and complex concept (Cuomo, 2003). It is because of this complexity that we have introduced historically marginalized groups separately, incorporating discussions of intersecting oppressions. The oppression of each group of people operates differently, but not separately. Ultimately, however, "studying oppressed groups in isolation is to marginalize much of the community" (Glenn, 1992, p. 3); such an approach creates a false picture by not taking into account the multiple layers and forms of oppression experienced by many people. In order to develop a full understanding of oppression and critical multicultural social work, one must understand how the categories of oppressed groups intersect (Mullaly, 2002). Assessing how the categories overlap and the additive nature of oppression allows a more accurate picture to emerge.

As we learned in previous chapters, a person's identity encompasses more than just the dimensions considered in models of individual development over the life span. Name, history, social status, gender and sex, ethnoracial identity, sexual orientation, ability status, income/socioeconomic status, education, and religion all come into play. It is our identities, and their association with certain attributes, stereotypes, and norms, that define how others see us. We live within a multiplicity of identities, which exist in a world where some identities have been used to justify inequalities (Baynton, 2001).

The context of diversity is a global one, one that affects each of us at home and abroad. In the United States, the social order is grounded in economic status, a mixture of income and class, and the myth that success is a based on merit (Kincheloe & Steinberg, 1997). The pervasiveness of this myth limits the ability of people with privilege to see the barriers obstructing people in the "other" categories. Sexual orientation, ability status, "race, class and gender combine to create a larger playing field with more options for some and a smaller, more limited field for others" (Kincheloe & Steinberg, 1997, p. 33).

These oppressions occur on a multilevel playing field that is not equal for all players (Kincheloe & Steinberg, 1997). While people of color make up more than two-thirds of the world population, the wealth resides in the hands of a few (usually white) people and countries. Half of the world's people suffer from malnutrition, four-fifths live in substandard housing, and more than two-thirds are illiterate. "The dominant group holds maximum power when the distinction between 'us' and 'them' is believed to be a fundamental, irreversible dissymmetry in which groups have little in common" (Brantlinger, 2001, p. 2). The creation of divisions between groups encourages competition.

Oppression is entrenched in the structure of most social and economic systems, which creates and maintains human systems of violence and exploitation at all levels (Cuomo, 2003). It is caused and sustained by a set of political, social, and economic factors and results in systemic inequality. The catastrophe of Hurricane Katrina is a good example of this systemic inequality: residents of New Orleans who were marginalized by race and class were more likely to live in vulnerable areas, and least likely to receive either the immediate assistance or the resources needed to rebuild (Pyles, 2006). Mechanisms such as these, which block access to resources and life opportunities, shape the lives of individuals and communities. Only a purposeful effort to end oppression and discrimination can reverse this system. Life in a multicultural society requires careful self-scrutiny, as well as examination of our attitudes and beliefs, their origins, and their impact on our daily activities (Marsh, 2004).

People who live with privilege may still experience hardship. They may wonder why painful events in their lives are less important than the oppression experienced by marginalized groups. Although the hardships they experience may be painful, they are not necessarily grounded in structural barriers that affect people in vital and limiting ways. To enter into an exploration of oppression, it is necessary to set aside personal hardships that are not grounded in structural barriers and consider the barriers facing people who do not have access to resources. This requires us to set aside our feelings about our personal histories of hardship and listen to others without defending ourselves.

The Intersection

Understanding people individually and collectively requires us to weave together the privilege and marginalization continuums. Growth occurs as we recognize that diversity exists within identity groups we consider to be the "other," worldviews offer the potential for growth, and people are interrelated and interconnected (Lum, 2003). The intersection model, which was developed by radical social workers from Canada, illustrates the distinctions between the different forms of oppression (for further discussion, see Baines, 2000; Mullaly, 2002; Weinman, 1984). Each form of oppression has unique sources, and each affects particular groups in different ways. Individuals may be oppressed in one respect, but privileged in another (Weinman, 1984). The privilege of whiteness may be mitigated by a person's socioeconomic status and lack of access to educational and economic resources. One group has the privilege in terms of access to resources, while others experience barriers that the privileged may not be able to see. One's location in the social order often determines one's access to power, privilege, and resources. A white male may experience privilege by virtue of his gender and race. At the same time, he may experience oppression because of his class, sexual orientation, ability, education, and/or religion.

Through self-reflection we can each come to recognize the impact of oppression and privilege. From this base, we can empathize with others who experience different dimensions of oppression and privilege. The case in box 6.1 illustrates a social work student's exploration of the oppression of racism and the impact of privilege in his own family system.

Box 6.1   A Student's Exploration of Racism

As I received the assignment, I knew it was going to be very interesting for both my family and myself. Our professor asked us to interview the oldest member of our family to determine how the family developed stereotypes about individuals and groups of people. The professor provided a list of questions for us to ask:

What are your views about race relations in the twenty-first century?

Did you have friends from other races as a child and young adult? Do you now have friends of another race?

When did you first become aware of race?

What messages about race did you receive from your family and community as a child?

How would you feel if I were to marry someone from a different race?

I knew this would be an interesting assignment because I was involved in an interracial relationship, and no one in my family knew about this relationship. Frankly, I was afraid to tell anyone. I sat at the dinner table at home too many times and listened to numerous family debates about different racial groups in our society. Early on in my life I had received a message that no one in our family should marry anyone outside our race.

I decided to make this assignment even more interesting by asking my African American girlfriend (whom I am considering marrying) to do the same with her family. I later realized that I was subconsciously trying to ease my guilt. I was hoping that my girlfriend's family was as close minded as mine. The taboo subject that we never explored as a couple was why I had not invited her home. I have, however, been to her home on several occasions. Her family asked me numerous questions about my family, but they remained silent on a significant question: Did my parents know that I was in an interracial relationship?

What my grandmother said during the interview was that "we should love everyone and people are people and we should treat everyone the same." She went on to say that she really did not know any "colored people." She said she learned about their existence when her family was visiting a city, and she mentioned to her mom how tan they were and wondered aloud if she could get that type of tan. My grandmother still remembers her mother's response and the fear in her mother's eyes; the message was "They are bad people, never talk to one, and never let them in your home because they will hurt you." My grandmother received cultural messages from her parents that gave her negative beliefs about people of color. She never questioned why they felt this way; she just passed these negative feelings down to her children, including my mother. My grandmother obeyed her parents, and from that moment on she never approached an African American. What she learned on her own about this group of people came from the media, and that information was mostly negative because of institutional racism. In her mind, people of color who succeeded got away from the "bad coloreds" and assimilated into the dominant culture.

When I asked her what would happen if I married an African American woman, she looked me in the eye and said that she knew I would never do something like that. I was her handsome Italian American grandson and I was going to marry a beautiful Italian woman and have many children. I did not want to disillusion and hurt my grandmother. I too have to be honest: I had not told her because I did not want to face my family's disapproval.

At that point, I told her that I have an African American girlfriend and I was considering asking her to marry me. My grandmother first thought I was joking. When she realized I was being honest, she sat in silence for a few moments. Finally, she shook her head and said that I was being selfish. I was not thinking about our family or the fact that if we had children, they would have a hard life. She told me to have fun with my girlfriend but just let her go when I leave college. I should then look for someone of my "own kind." This was one of the code phrases from the list that my professor gave us entitled "When You Know You Have Met a Bigot."

I could not believe that my grandmother, whom I loved so much, was a bigot. She did not ask me if I was happy or if I loved this woman; she just wanted me to get over it. Instead of being angry at her, I realized that our family had never examined the issue of race and how it has affected us. I told my mom about my relationship and the conversation I had with her mother. She listened but she also did not encourage my relationship. I was really angry at my mom. I shouted that she taught her children to treat all people the same. All through our childhood she had insisted that our family was accepting of others. She marched us to church each Sunday and sent us to Catholic school for twelve years, and the message was always the same: "Love thy neighbor." It was a commandment from God. "Are we hypocrites?" was the final question that I asked her.

What I learned from this assignment is not a surprise. My family is very bigoted. Once "the race elephant in the room" was discussed openly, I discovered the biggest surprise of all: I was a passive racist. I realized that I was liberal regarding race as long as people of color thought like me. I now must admit I was just tolerant of people of color and ignored the fact that I needed to change and become more self-aware and open in order to explore racial differences. I should have been open about my interracial relationship and willing to question my family values. I should have forced my family to consider why we are racist.

I now understand why people of color do not trust the majority. Most whites are conditioned to say the politically correct thing, but we are really afraid to explore why racism exists. We must grapple with the hard fact that whites as a group of people are either overtly or covertly racist. As Peggy McIntosh (1990) states, we are privileged and we need to "unpack our knapsacks." Are we ever going to demand social justice for all people?

I am in a relationship that I should have shared with my family. I should have discussed with them the ups and downs of loving someone who is different. I kept this secret to myself. I knew all along that my family would not be supportive when I shared my news. I am disappointed in them, but I am even more deeply disappointed in myself.

This assignment also helped me understand Janet Helms's white identity model. I was so naive, and I have a lot of personal work to do to dispel my beliefs about other groups of people. I love my girlfriend. I now have questions, and I have made a commitment to address them. I am on what will be a lifelong quest to understand the complex issues of racism. My girlfriend and I have committed to work hard as a couple, not hiding from the issues concerning race that we confront in our relationship.

As a person who is entering the social work profession, I must embrace the NASW Code of Ethics by becoming more aware of why I do the things that I do. This is critical if I wish to help others. I hate what I found out about myself and my family, but what would have happened if I had never discovered this? If I had failed to do this, how could I help people from different cultural backgrounds as a social worker? How could I become culturally competent?

Previously, as I sat in class and heard students of color telling their stories, I dismissed those stories by telling myself it was not my fault; I did not do anything to contribute to the plight of African Americans. Thinking honestly about this is difficult. I understand why white students are reluctant to speak up; it is hard to process these things. It is time, however, that we do so if we, as future social workers, want to develop the skills necessary to help those who are living with racism and among racist people. I look forward to working hard to become a better person and a better social worker by truly examining these "isms."

Oppressions, however, "intersect at innumerable points in everyday life and are mutually reinforcing, creating a total system of oppression in which one continuum of stratification cannot be addressed in isolation from all others" (Weinman, 1984, p. 169). This intersection creates a kind of web. Within the web, oppressions overlap; they are not hierarchical nor are they additive; rather, they are cumulative. The web in figure 6.1 is one representation of the intersecting web of oppressions. The groups in the center are those with institutionalized privilege. As you look at the wheel, evaluate the ways in which power and privilege are distributed.

A Latino man may have gender/sex privilege but experience ethnoracial oppression. An African American man with economic resources has more options than one who does not have those resources. Class can be a major factor. One's accent may intersect with class, resulting in stigma and isolation. People's internalized views of what is normal lead to assumptions about individuals and groups. For instance, many people with privilege assume that all African Americans come from a background of poverty. In fact, the majority of African Americans do not live in poverty. Middle-class status can alleviate some of the negative effects of ethnoracial oppression by providing access to resources such as health care, housing, education, child care, and transportation (Mullaly, 2002). The case in box 6.2 offers an example of a worker who made assumptions based on preconceived ideas about race and culture, combined with a lack of knowledge about the client as well as his family and community. These assumptions interfered with her ability to observe, listen, and engage respectfully and knowledgeably with the client and his family.

Box 6.2   An Older African American Adult

My father was in the end stages of kidney disease and needed to have dialysis three times a week. The hospital social worker suggested that unless a family member could take my father full time, we should consider placing him in the county nursing home. She told me not to worry or feel guilty; she knew that his children needed to work. She expressed her concern that we should not feel that we had to take on this financial hardship.

FIGURE 6.1   The Web

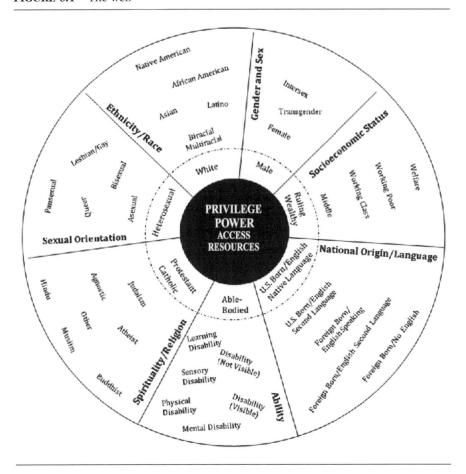

The social worker's role was to develop the best discharge plan for my father. The social worker said she would help our family apply for welfare and medical assistance to help defray the cost of the nursing home. She also said that it would be helpful if we could obtain copies of all our financial statements in order to establish that we could not help financially. If we were proactive and got all the paperwork together, she could establish that we were not able to help. She wanted my dad to receive all the benefits that he was entitled to. She stated that everything would be "smooth sailing" since she was "100 percent certain" that dad was eligible for many of the social programs and nursing home placement based on need.

The social worker went on to say she felt my father may also have early signs of dementia since he did not seem to be lucid at times. I was surprised to hear this, since neither the doctor nor I had noticed any signs of this. Reluctantly, I asked her how she came to this conclusion. The social worker responded slowly, allowing me time to comprehend. She reported that he was unable to recall information regarding his life. She went on to say that when she interviewed my father and asked him some questions about his life, he rambled. I asked her to be patient with me and reconstruct her conversation with my dad, as that would help me to understand.

She smiled when she said my father reminded her of an old African American family friend whom she called "Pops." Pops was employed by her parents to maintain the gardens and fix things at her home. She saw my father as a cute elderly African American man, and she felt it was okay to call my Dad "Pops." I grimaced but did not let her see it. In our family we were taught to call anyone older than us "Mister" or "Missus." I wondered why this social worker felt free to call my dad "Pops."

She said that my father said he was married and that he attended and graduated from the Mecca. He talked about Jack and Jill, the Links, and the Ques. He also told her he was a knight. He told her that he was ready for his homecoming but had hoped that he could stay in his own home until it was his time. At that point she said he was not making much sense. She said she asked him a few follow-up questions to get the information she needed, but he seemed to get frustrated and agitated, so she decided to end the interview.

I knew exactly what the problem was as soon as she gave me this information. Do you? Let's review just a few of the critical issues the social worker made assumptions about and therefore failed to explore.

First, the worker did not follow the golden rule: she did not use the strengths perspective, and she failed to empower the client and his family. It is evident that the worker's intention was to work in the client's best interest, but her ability to do this was obstructed by the stereotypes she held about people of color and older adults. She never asked the client or his family if they felt the client needed any financial assistance. The worker needed to ask probing questions to determine whether the family was in a position to offer either emotional or financial support. The social worker just assumed that they were emotionally supportive but did not have the time or the funds to assist their father. She failed to talk with all parties about how the father and the family felt about alternate placements or aging in place (staying in his own home).

The social worker made several assumptions that narrowed the scope of her assessment. Remember that the worker stated that this gentleman reminded her of someone from her past. She somehow determined that this man was of the lower socioeconomic status, perhaps just like the family friend named Pops. She even felt that she had the right (white privilege behavior) to call him by this other man's name. In essence, the worker failed to ask what help the family wanted, what resources were available, or how she should address the father.

Third, she went so far as to state that she felt the father was experiencing dementia. She assumed that information that didn't make sense to her was a sign of dementia. She misunderstood words and phrases related to the African American experience. Had she used her lack of knowledge as a base to engage the family in discussion, she would have learned what the terms used by the father meant. Although no one person can know everything about another race or culture, the worker failed to ask others if the father's "babble" meant something to them. Unfortunately the worker just assumed this was a symptom of dementia, which caused her client and his family great frustration. When the client referred to the Mecca, he was referring to Howard University, a historically black institution in Washington, D.C. Jack and Jill and the Links are social organizations that African American families join to develop a strengths perspective about African American history, culture, and socialization opportunities. Both of these organizations provide numerous networks for members. Many middle- and upper-class African Americans are members of Jack and Jill and Links. When the father referred to himself as a Que, this meant that he was a member of Omega Psi Phi, a national African American fraternity for men. When he said he was a knight, he was referring to yet another organization, the Knights of Columbus, which is a Catholic fraternal benefit organization. Many African Americans use the word "homecoming" as a euphemism to refer to one's time to die and go to heaven.

Had the worker listened without making assumptions, she would have had a base of questions for gathering information. As she filled in the gaps, she would have learned that the father attended and graduated from a university. She would also have learned that his social circle was vast, since he was affiliated with numerous social organizations. The father could have enough caring people in his social network to age in place. Finally, and most importantly, she would have explored whether or not the father and his children had a financial plan that would allow them to provide the resources he needed.

The most important lesson to remember from this is that you must use all your social work skills with all your clients. Although the worker would have learned about the family's finances once the family filled out the forms, she could never repair the harm that was done to the helping relationship. Most importantly, in order to work with individuals from different cultures and backgrounds, it is essential that social workers understand different cultures and are culturally competent. Successful client outcomes and effective social work practice are dependent on an understanding of difference.

Young's five faces of oppression (exploitation, marginalization, powerlessness, cultural imperialism, and violence) operate across marginalized groups. Though individuals in all groups face hardships and barriers, every person does not experience the structural barriers of oppression in the same way. The form of oppression may vary, yet individuals in communities of oppressed groups are affected by mechanisms that isolate and marginalize. Exploring the mechanisms of oppression can help us clarify and magnify the ways in which a group is privileged and/or the ways in which members of that group are oppressed.

In the same way that the dimensions of oppression overlap, so do the mechanisms used to maintain oppression. These mechanisms of oppression are the means for maintaining an unbalanced social order. Social and economic systems exploit some groups, thus keeping them marginalized. In work, education, housing, and health care, some groups are privileged, while others experience the powerlessness that comes with marginalization. This is exacerbated by the cultural imperialism that overtly or covertly centers the privileged group as normal and sees other groups as the "other." Mechanisms of violence and intimidation frighten and reinforce oppression, causing people to impose limitations on themselves. For instance, women limit their behavior because of the fear of rape. This is a personal concern for the individual and also a fear that is perpetuated by the media and social structures. Dismantling the mechanisms of oppression requires us to work together rather than in isolation. The interplay between the individual and social and economic systems makes it necessary to engage in multilevel change.

Position

Each of us is positioned in a particular context in terms of race/ethnicity, class, gender and sex, and ability at our birth and/or adoption. This positioning is not a matter of choice. Our positions in the gender/sex, ethnoracial, class, and ability continuums provide an indicator of our status. Our positions can transform over time as we grow and change; this creates the potential for multiple identities.

The web in figure 6.1 provides a model for examining one's position at the intersections of class, sex and gender, race, religion, ability, and sexual orientation. Exploration of these intersections and Maher and Tetreatult's (1993) concept of position or positionality are an aid for further developing an understanding of oppression. The center of the web represents access to resources. Those at the center in each wedge have privilege in that dimension. As we move away from the center, those farthest from the center do not necessarily have less access to resources than those who are closer to the center but outside the ring of privilege. For instance, Native Americans are not necessarily more oppressed than African Americans. In some cases, though, those positioned farther from the center do encounter more obstacles to accessing resources. For example, a transgender individual may experience more isolation and stigma than an intersex individual. Or a person receiving public assistance may experience more stigma than one who is working but poor.

Sometimes privilege is a person's internalized assumption of normality and her or his inability to see obstacles. For instance, on the sexual orientation continuum, most people view heterosexuality as normal. This results in the assumption that all others are not normal. If we cannot see the barriers created by these assumptions, then we cannot move beyond placing blame on the individuals and communities that encounter them. In recognizing and acknowledging obstacles, we begin to see possibilities for joining as allies to oppressed groups to dismantle these barriers.

Create a web by drawing a line to connect your positions across the wedges. Situate yourself in each section of the wheel according to your position at birth and/or adoption. Use a different color to situate yourself in the web based on your current positioning. Multiple mappings can represent change or provide a representation of uniformity. Examine the intersection between dimensions of oppression.

Now imagine the barriers that are created when one occupies multiple positions far from the core of the web. An individual, family, or community experiencing ethnoracial and socioeconomic oppression encounters multiple barriers. Gender and race form another intersection. While they have historically constituted separate fields of inquiry, the concepts of race and gender depend on each other. These two dimensions are so closely intertwined in individuals that it is impossible to separate the intertwining impact into separate spheres. We cannot understand gender without reference to race, nor can we consider race without considering gender (White, 2001). In addition to the oppressions of race and gender, women of color who have a low socioeconomic status experience oppression at the intersections of race, class, and gender. "As different forms of oppression are added to an already oppressive situation, the interactions increase exponentially, which in turn, increase the complexity of oppression on a person" (Mullaly, 2000, p. 155).

The Web: Yesterday, Today, and Tomorrow

A person's position at birth can be very different from her or his current and future positions. One's social and economic position may change, or there may be changes in health status, which can make navigating the life course more or less difficult. A person may develop a clearer understanding of her or his sexual orientation and gender identity as she or he ages, which can disturb assumptions of normality. Position on the multicultural spectrum influences social, political, and economic options. Age, class, religion, and national origin intersect with sex, gender, race, and sexual orientation. As Tatum (2003) says, "Constructing our identities is a complex process for all of us, but for some it is more complicated than for others" (p. 167). Some of the theories on multiracial identity development explore this complexity and the impact of overlapping identities.

The factor model of multiracial identity presented by Wijeyesinghe (2001) and discussed in chapter 2 identifies eight factors that affect the development of racial identity of multiracial people in the United States: cultural attachment, early experience and socialization, political awareness and orientation, spirituality, racial ancestry, physical appearance, social and historical context, and other social identities.

Context at Birth/Adoption

The position into which we are born is one over which we have no control; it is the context in which one finds oneself (Schultz, 1970). We do not have a choice of either our parents or our social circumstances. We are thrown into a world in which the expectations of the structures and people around us mold our roles and behavior (Young, 2000). One day we awake into a context—family, culture, language, ethnoracial identity, class status, country of birth and/or adoption, and sex, and physical and mental ability; it is assumed that our gender matches our sex and that we are heterosexual. We are thrown into a web of interactions that are strongly influenced by our social positions (Freire, 1997). We might be thrown into poverty; we might be thrown into wealth. Our class, gender and sex, ethnoracial identity, nationality, sexual orientation, and religion are not a choice. Our job is to adjust (Young, 1990).

If one is born white, there are privileges bestowed by that identity; if one is born a person of color, these privileges are not available. If one is male, there are privileges; if one is presumed heterosexual, there are privileges; if one is able-bodied, there are privileges. Class and income cut across the other variables, mediating the impact of oppression for individuals and communities with resources, and limiting access for communities and individuals from privileged groups who do not have class privilege. In each category there is a position that is considered normal. If one is not in this group, one is seen as the "other" and is subject to the oppressions of marginalization, exploitation, powerlessness, cultural imperialism, and possibly violence.

The Transformative Impact of Self-Exploration

The process of developing self-knowledge is difficult (Marsh, 2004). Exploring the self, including one's hidden privileges and oppressions, opens new doors for participation in critical multicultural practice. The transformative process shifts and broadens worldviews. While it is important to understand the negative impact of oppression, it is also vital to explore and appreciate the strengths and triumphs of traditionally oppressed groups. As we begin to listen to the voices of all people, we can learn from different worldviews, values, customs, family styles, and social structures. "Human diversity calls for discovery, learning, and understanding of each other" (Lum, 2003, p. 36). "When the spaces of difference are explored deeply and reflexively, then any one space may not seem so different from another. Yet . . . exploration of the spaces of difference cannot begin until we are able to hear the voices that come from those spaces" (Washington & Harris, 2001, p. 82). This exploration of the differences and similarities within and between groups provides a base for examining individual, family, and community strengths and hardships. True learning moves beyond essentializing—seeing all people in a group as identical—and involves a critical understanding of how social stratification and unequal access to resources affect individuals and groups within various groups and communities. Each individual, and each family, is different. Understanding ourselves and our experiences offers "an opportunity to build bridges of understanding across differences based on an acceptance and appreciation of what it means to be unique human beings" (Lum, 2003, p. 34).

Isolation and invisibility obscure many qualities that enable people to survive oppression. Hidden strengths and individual and community resilience are overlooked. Those with controlling access to the media and educational system often silence voices that acknowledge the strengths, resilience, and possibilities. Developing resilience by overcoming obstacles builds strengths, a form of inoculation against future adversity that enhances skills for coping with life's adversities.

The imperative for social workers to engage in the process of self-exploration is professionally sanctioned. The National Association of Social Workers (2001) has ten standards for culturally competent practice, one of which charges social workers with the responsibility of developing an awareness of self. Without this awareness, they would be ill prepared to engage with clients in a multicultural environment. Standard 2, on self-awareness, reads as follows: "Social workers shall seek to develop an understanding of their own personal, cultural values and beliefs as one way of appreciating the importance of multicultural identities in the lives of people" (National Association of Social Workers, 2001, p. 1).

Cultural competence requires an understanding of one's own worldview and also those of the individuals and communities with whom one is working. The social worker who is skilled in cross-cultural work recognizes and values the differences between these worldviews without negative judgment and assumptions of normality (Sue & Sue, 1999). She or he is able to critically evaluate and challenge the dominant cultural worldview. Self-awareness and critical reflectivity are used to examine one's own behavior and motivation and to understand the contexts within which people of different backgrounds experience their lives. It is critical that social workers understand, respect, and appreciate cultural differences in worldviews. Social workers who are culturally skilled explore the ways in which race and ethnicity, gender and sex, sexual orientation, income/class, and ability affect identity development, educational and employment choices, health and mental health, and requests for assistance. They are then able to determine which intervention approaches are appropriate.

Critically engaged and self-reflective social workers take this understanding and translate it into direct action for social change. They work together with individuals and communities in a process of empowerment and a process of transforming society into an equitable and just system for all community members. Social workers with a critical awareness of how cultural ideology fosters social injustice and inequity have an improved ability to work with clients and communities. This work contributes to the dismantling of oppressive cultural values as well as systemic inequities.

Chapter 7

Arenas for Critical Multicultural Practice

Social workers who are committed to social justice must join the struggle against oppression in all its forms and at all levels at which it occurs.

Bob Mullaly, *Challenging Oppression*

History is filled with calculated and sometimes brutal instances of exclusions of people of color, women, people who are GLBT, and people who are disabled. Systemized sexism, racism, homophobia and heterosexism, ableism, transphobia, and classism continue to be a problem in society. These conditions affect communities, the lives of clients, the daily practice of social work, and social workers on multiple levels. The barriers are structural, limiting access to education, employment, housing, and health care. Social and economic policies maintain this limited access, and social systems reinforce the inequality by failing to recognize or acknowledge oppressive structures and assumptions of normality. As a result, individuals, families, and communities face roadblocks that can forestall growth and create stress in relationships. This unequal access to opportunities has an intergenerational impact because future generations cannot build on the successes of their parents and grandparents.

Oppressive social patterns permeate our communities, organizations, and interpersonal relationships. Failure to disrupt these mechanisms is to lose one's basic humanity (Mullaly, 2002). In growing to understand our own culture and community and its impact upon our experiences of oppression and privilege, we can begin the process of change. This is a change that begins at the individual and global levels simultaneously.

Critical multicultural practice is anti-oppression practice. It is a form of practice that is grounded in "issues of representation and democratic inclusiveness with its roots in the relationship between politics and power, within the context of a historical past and a living present" (Van Soest, 2003, p. 345), and the hope of a more inclusive future. The development and implementation of social and economic policies have consequences that affect individuals.

Societal values underlie policy decisions. In the United States, poverty rates are high, individualism and competition are valued, and individuals experiencing poverty are viewed negatively. In a society such as Norway, on the other hand, collectivity and cooperation are valued and poverty rates are low. The Norwegian value base supports "(1) egalitarianism and the collective ideal, (2) trust in the social system, and (3) kindness toward the weak and vulnerable" (van Wormer, 1994, p. 325). The value base underlying the development of policy in the United States can be recast to support a commitment to the collective well-being and egalitarianism. The interplay between social and economic policy, the communities in which we live, the media, the organizations in which we work, and our families demands a multilevel response. While working toward policies that are socially and economically just, we must also heal our communities, reorganize the organizations in which we work, and support the individuals and families that are wounded by unresponsive or ineffective systems.

Because people exist within environments, healing is contextual. A new narrative that recognizes the impact of oppression and sets the stage for healing internalized oppression must be constructed. Individual, family, and community characteristics can buffer the impact of adversity. In recognizing the similarities and differences between individuals, one values the uniqueness of each human being. "Certainly this attitude and approach to people as particular persons is the beginning of cultural competence" (Lum, 2003, p. 34).

Social work is a profession that acknowledges that "people should be perceived not only as individuals, but also as members of social groups and cultures affected by the social, economic, and political conditions in which they live" (Kahn, 1991, p. 2). This orientation becomes increasingly important as the diversity of the population in the United States grows. This means learning to listen, and listening to learn about how lives are shaped. It means learning how others view family, community, and themselves, and learning how people cope with adversity and success. Within this context social workers need to develop an appreciation for the interaction between resiliency and oppression (Long & Nelson, 1999).

Intersecting Differences

Individuals, families, and communities do not exist in a vacuum or in isolation. Within each is a complex intersection of identities involving ethnoracial group, gender and sex, and sexual orientation as well as ability, economic resources, history, language, nationality, and religion. Just practice requires the worker to acknowledge and understand "the intersection and complex interaction of multiple social identities and a continuum of harm and privilege that confer these identities" (Van Soest, 2003, p. 345).

The multicultural mosaic is a constantly changing one. Contact between cultures, traditions, and beliefs has resulted in a blending of cultures, and the formation of new cultures. Traditional ways of being and knowing are honored while the elements of the dominant group that are necessary for survival are embraced. Conversely, members of the dominant culture adopt the traditions of marginalized communities, which gives them a glimpse of the world of the "other." Embracing traditional elements of the "other" alters one's worldview, creating opportunities to examine one's own values and beliefs. Some members of communities of color hold steadfast to traditional ways that both support and nurture members; other members of communities of color embrace a more Eurocentric worldview and have been able to flourish and maintain a unique cultural identity. As one engages in practice, it is vital to honor the individual and her or his complexity, acknowledging the intricacies of community, culture, and history.

Policy and Community

Social problems in the United States and the human misery they create continue to arise. Although it is the responsibility of the government to promote the well-being of all citizens, responses to these problems are increasingly inadequate as the growth of wealth becomes more and more concentrated among the few (Kahn, 1991). "The wealthiest 1 percent of the American population holds 38 percent of the total national wealth. . . . The richest 20 percent of Americans hold 83 percent of the total household wealth in the country. . . . Approximately 12 percent of the American population—one in every eight people in this country lives below the official poverty line. . . . Among the poor are over 2.3 million homeless, including nearly 1 million homeless children. Approximately one out of every five children in the United States under the age of six lives in poverty" (Mantsios, 2004, p. 195). As the division grows ever wider, we must ask not only who is left out, but also why.

Collective action can disrupt the negative impact of the social and economic policies confronting marginalized communities (Kahn, 1991). The process offers the potential for growth by providing an opportunity for people to find their voices, develop collectivity and skills, and create hope. As individuals work together toward community change, individual and relational dynamics are restructured. Individuals are empowered as they advocate change. In the process, worldviews, relationship patterns, and personal potential are altered.

Caring, compassion, and spiritual commitment produce powerful emotions for motivating change. A renewed sense of hope is engendered as collective action engages the social and political process through advocacy, organizing, and community building. Organizing creates an environment in which individuals and communities can learn to share power and work toward empowerment (Kahn, 1991). While this can be challenging, it can also lead to the development of comradeship and collective empowerment as social justice values are translated into practice.

Mullaly (2002) asserts that "If, in our personal lives and in our social work practice, we assist in making oppression acceptable by helping people to cope with it or adjust to it, we not only fail them, we fail ourselves and we become part of the problem" (p. 211). Effective practice with individuals and communities of color requires social workers to address macropractice issues (McPhatter, 1997). Likewise, macropractice techniques are effective with other oppressed communities. This involves the use of interventions with systems, organizations, and service providers. The ability to organize has always been empowering for women. WomanSpirit of St. Louis, Missouri, offers a model for organizing and mobilizing African American women to influence policies locally, nationally, and globally (Prince, 1999). They work across generations, providing resources and fostering empowerment at the individual and community levels. Organizations such as this exemplify the phrase "The personal is political."

Practice with Individuals and Families: Understanding Community Context

Culture, class, resources, and social context are critical elements that shape struggles and affect an individual's ability to develop coping resources (Devore & Schlesinger, 1998). These interactions influence the development of individual, family, and community worldviews (Lum, 2003). Family and community class roots interact with the income, education, and lifestyle of an individual. The interchange is a complex one in which strengths frequently intermingle with fears and vulnerabilities. Situational interchanges, historical and cultural influences, and the interpretation of experiences affect the construction of meaning, vision, and perception.

A thorough assessment of individual, family, and community culture allows practitioners to begin to explore appropriate models of practice. Racism, classism, sexism, homophobia and heterosexism, transphobia, ableism, and other forms of discrimination and oppression are a part of our lives and therefore must be considered for their possible effects on people's lives (Lum, 2003). The rise in nationalism in the United States is increasingly isolating for the country (Friedman, 2006). The accompanying anti-immigrant feelings create a negative environment that social workers need to be aware of when working with refugees and other immigrants.

An ethnoracial assessment involves a clarification of the client's (and worker's) interpretation of the significance of events and their meaning for the client, which decreases the possibility that the worker will miss vital information (Jenkins, 1988). This exploration of identity is key to understanding the multicultural context and environment of individual and familial functioning, group identity and membership, broad value perspectives, and sources of strength and stress. By acknowledging and understanding the historical and structural dimensions of racism, classism, and other forms of oppression, a practitioner can engage in the critical reflective process. Kondrat (1999) recommends two levels of questioning to assist in this process. First, ask global questions:

1. What are the structures of my society in particular that are related to power and inequality and marginalization?
2. On what basis are these structures rationalized by society?
3. What is my location in relation to each of these structures?

4. Who benefits from such structural arrangements, and who loses? How do I benefit or lose?
5. In what ways do my assumptions and activities contribute to the maintenance and/or transformation of such social structures?
6. What have I discovered about the extended structural consequences of my social activities and that of others? (p. 465)

Next, ask questions about your own cultural assumptions and worldviews. What are your values and beliefs and your interpretations of your world, and what are those of people who are different from you? How do these beliefs affect your actions and interactions between yourself and others? Social workers who engage in this reflective process are better equipped to help clients move through a similar process as one component of healing.

A process of self-assessment can assist clients in recognizing their own assumptions, beliefs, and values, along with the changes they desire (McMillen, 1999). The individual is the creator of the story that is told. The social worker only facilitates the telling of the story. Leigh's (1998) ethnographic interview is one tool that can be used to guide this process. The ethnographic interview supports an interactive process of learning about the individual within her or his context. It begins with a global exploration of culture and history and then comes to focus on the individual. Personal and family history, multilevel resilience factors, and experiences of abuse and trauma are evaluated. Individual, family, and community strengths and resources are assessed. The process of building rapport opens a window to the client's worldview and cultural interpretation of events.

The models of practice used must be congruent with the client's dimensions of difference, community values, and worldview. For instance, individualistic models of practice are incompatible with the focus on extended family and community connections in many indigenous cultures (Weaver, 1999). Interventions that build from systems theory, emphasize the social environment, and embrace the strengths perspective often are a better fit for oppressed populations (see Lum, 2003, for a presentation of treatment models).

Feminist models and other critical models of practice incorporate an awareness of the types of oppression faced by women and other communities (Appleby et al., 2001). These models support practice that assists clients in understanding the role of both social constraints and opportunities in shaping their lives (Garnets & Peplau, 2001). Social workers must be aware of and sensitive to the issues faced by the different groups with whom they work. These issues have an effect on daily living, personal adjustment, access to resources, and coping mechanisms.

People who are members of oppressed groups are affected by societal and professional attitudes, biases, and actions. For example, transgender individuals may be coping with feelings of guilt, shame, fear, anxiety, low self-esteem, anger, and isolation as a result of societal intolerance. They bring with them family history (positive and negative), personal trauma, interactions with social networks, adjustment issues, and possibly depression and addictive behaviors. A social worker's comfort with and knowledge of the issues faced by transgender clients are significant determinants of the quality of interaction. The issues are exaggerated for people of color who are transgender (Gainor, 2000).

Working with refugees and other immigrants means recognizing the multi-layered loss experienced by refugees and other immigrants of friends, family, language, and general comfort. For refugees, this is often compounded by a history of terror and multiple displacements (Devore & Schlesinger, 1998; Schmitz, Vazquez Jacobus, Stakeman, Valenzuela, & Sprankel, 2003). The loss is exacerbated further for refugees and other immigrants who are women, particularly those of color (Lie & Lowery, 2003). These women must redefine themselves within a Eurocentric context. This involves negotiating new surroundings with unfamiliar sights and sounds, interactional patterns, social relationships, structural forces, and language patterns. Refugee women have the "added burdens of issues emanating from the horrors of war, forced migration, and relocation" (Lie & Lowery, 2003, p. 299). Families from immigrant and refugee communities entering new lives in the United States are at risk of traumatic adjustment. Federal policies impact them directly and indirectly, privileging some while challenging others. "It is incumbent upon social workers, as professionals committed to social and economic justice, to comprehensively understand the range of obstacles facing immigrants and refugees and empower them in their struggle to make a healthy adjustment" (Schmitz et al., 2003, p. 135). At the same time, immigrant and refugee women of color can find strength and rewards within the new cultural context. Women from some communities find that in the United States they have greater equality in gendered relations. This change has an impact on individuals as well as communities. Family relationships can change, and depression can follow as men lose their privilege.

The ableist attitudes of society also affect social workers. As a result of these attitudes, social workers may underestimate the capabilities of individuals with disabilities, which may limit the options workers envision for their clients (Mackelprang & Salsgiver, 1999).

Assessment and Practice from a Critical Perspective

Critical assessment and practice involves building knowledge regarding historical and social policy views, ecological as well as ethnoracial and class contexts, and feminist and other anti-oppression perspectives. Ecological assessment sets the stage for informed response, providing an outline for evaluation of the dimensions of personal and structural oppression experienced by clients. Through anti-oppression practice, clients are engaged in tasks that help them remediate the damage created by oppression while also creating solidarity by building community (Mullaly, 2002). The triumph experienced by the client engaged in the social change process builds strength.

Walters, Longres, Han, and Icard (2003) state, "A key skill [in culturally competent practice] is the ability to take the role of others, that is, to see the world from the standpoint of one's clients, and from that position, to work with them and their communities to improve their lives and their social and economic conditions" (pp. 329–330). Social constructivist theory supports this model of practice by framing analysis around how clients make sense of the activities and events in their world. The interchange between people and their environmental, cultural, and historical contexts is emphasized by social constructivist theory. Understanding this interchange between a person and her or his environment, and the meanings she or he attaches to that interchange, is critical to a meaningful assessment (Mallon, 1999b). The strengths-based and narrative models of practice build from the social constructivist theory and enable this process.

Strengths and Empowerment

The strengths-based model is recognized as suitable for practice with individuals, families, and communities of color (Devore & Schlesinger, 1998). This model provides an opportunity to view individuals, situations, and environments from a perspective of possibility and resilience (Saleebey, 2002). The impact of adversity is heavily influenced by a person's resilience. Multiple factors on the individual, family, and community levels support the development of resilience. This knowledge is critical in work with marginalized populations. Cultural connections and positive racial pride are dimensions of resilience (Lafromboise, Coleman, & Gerton, 1993; Miller & MacIntosh, 1999). For instance, "resiliency in Native American communities involves an interdependence of factors that are relational rather than linear" (Long & Nelson, 1999, p. 104). In indigenous communities, positive cultural identification and participation in traditional events buffer the impact of adversity (Waller & Yellow Bird, 2002). Similarly, positive identity development in lesbians and gay men of color can buffer the stresses of heterosexism and homophobia, sexism, and racism (Walters et al., 2003). Identifying resilience and survival strategies in individuals, families, and communities of reference facilitates the development of coping strategies and supports growth.

Strengths-based practice is focused on exploring opportunities, capabilities, capacities, and possibilities (Mackelprang & Salsgiver, 1999). It is an affirming model of practice that fosters discovery and growth. Workers help clients engage in the exploration and reinforcement of strengths with the goal of developing and realizing dreams (Saleebey, 2002). For instance, models of strength combined with supportive practice environments are vital in work with transgender children and youths (Mallon, 1999b). These lessons are significant for work with the broader lesbian, gay, bisexual, and transgender communities, as well as other marginalized and stigmatized communities. When working with persons with disabilities, the social worker might work individually and collectively, empowering individuals by encouraging involvement in community and policy change (Mackelprang & Salsgiver, 1999). Individual strengths are nurtured, while environmental resources and community responsiveness are increased.

Through the empowerment process, individuals and groups that previously saw themselves as powerless are supported as they engage in collaborative change. The expansion of supportive environments, identification of resources, provision of training, and development of mechanisms for addressing social stigmatization and oppression are components of empowerment practice (Mallon, 1999c). Assessment, as well as intervention, is grounded in multilevel knowledge about the personal and systemic/structural issues. Stories are retold from a position of strength and resistance, rather than from a position of isolation and assimilation (Walters et al., 2003).

Increased awareness regarding the forces of oppression fuels the process of growth (Appleby et al., 2001). Personal narratives become a tool for supporting the development of the skills needed to acquire control (Tully, 2000). This is a visioning approach that incorporates individual, community, and neighborhood resources and strengths (Mackelprang & Salsgiver, 1999). The provision of advocacy and the alleviation of isolation and depression through community action empower individuals and communities. This dual focus on the individual and issues of social and economic justice strengthens marginalized communities (Appleby et al., 2001).

Narrative and Story

Narrative practice builds from the theory of social construction (Holland & Kilpatrick, 1993). Life stories are shared in interactions between the social worker and the client (Lum, 2003). Narrative and storying emphasize strengths, providing the base for a positive approach to practice (Saleebey, 1994). Stories can build bridges to connect communities, and therefore the use of stories in social work practice supports multicultural practice (Holland & Kilpatrick, 1993). Narrative practice occurs as the social worker and client explore the client's stories about cultural myths, rituals, and concerns from which people, families, and communities construct meaning.

Stories and storytelling are methods for creating, sustaining, and transmitting meaning (Holland & Kilpatrick, 1993). Because meaning is socially constructed through exchange and interchange, storying provides a venue for the social worker to facilitate change. The collaborative exploration of stories offers individuals, families, and communities the possibility to restory, reframe, and reorganize the narrative so that it becomes one of empowerment. As Saleebey (1994) notes, "Meaning, whether manifested in story, narrative, vision, or language, affects intention and action, feeling and mood, relationships, interactions with the surrounding world, well-being, and possibility" (p. 355).

Reflection on the stories people tell allows workers to increase their understanding of the client's worldview and life experience (Holland & Kilpatrick,

1993).The highlighting of positive life experiences and supportive relationships and interactions helps the client focus on success and her or his potential.The practitioner assumes an interpretive role by listening, identifying themes, and reflecting on clients' reactions to events and their stories. Sensitivity facilitates the process of reconstructing the story (Holland & Kilpatrick, 1993).

Narrative and storying support a process that allows us to modify or broaden worldviews, acknowledge multiple perspectives, and alter interactions with others (McMillen, 1999). Because adversity can leave people with feelings of guilt and shame, supporting people in building more positive and empowering memories of negative events facilitates the process of growth. Positive associations allow people to view painful memories from a different perspective. Facing adversity, recognizing the potential for growth, building self-esteem, and viewing oneself as capable creates resilience. Recalling memories of successful coping helps people embrace the totality of their experience, not just the pain.

Through restorying, lesbian, gay, and bisexual individuals, as well as their families, can build self-esteem, an internal sense of worth and value, and a vision of a future with positive possibilities. Practice with lesbians and gay men involves learning the significance of the coming-out story and the impact of homophobia and heterosexism (Pearlmutter, 1999). It also means respecting individual and family choice regarding the process. Reframing is also empowering in helping lesbians and gay men of color stop feeling caught between four communities (the gay or lesbian community, the ethnoracial community, one's gender group, and the community of gay or lesbian people of color) and appreciate and take advantage of the opportunity to act as a cultural bridge (Walters et al., 2003).

Organizational Context

Culturally effective practice must occur in all activities and at all levels of an organization (McPhatter & Ganaway, 2003). Key leaders within the organization set the tone, and their support is crucial as commitment to becoming critically multicultural is rallied. The process of transformation is supported through structural and environmental change, along with training and knowledge building. Spaces designed to be inclusive of marginalized populations tend to display an overall welcoming environment.These organizations are also likely to exhibit a commitment to advocacy and community change.

Culturally responsive supervisors are key to critical multicultural practice. A collaborative reflective process helps supervisors recognize cultural positions and biases, and collective learning through storytelling helps supervisors foster cultural competence among workers (Abt-Perkins, Hauschildt, & Dale, 2000). Through this process, supervisors and workers come to examine their blind spots, fears, and silences.

A knowledge of organizational dynamics and a multisystem process guide organizational transformation (McPhatter, 1997; Mallon, 1999a). McPhatter and

Ganaway (2003) outline five stages in the change process: pre-contemplation, contemplation, preparation, action, and maintenance. The methods of engagement shift with each stage. Pre-contemplation requires education about the issues regarding different cultures and populations. In the contemplation stage, the problem is identified and dialogue regarding change begins; the plan for change is outlined and engaged in the preparation phase. In the action phase, the change begins in earnest. Finally, in the last stage, maintenance, the change is solidified.

Conclusion

The skills and knowledge essential for critical multicultural social work support enriched practice with all populations. Effective practice is holistic, taking into account the totality of context and identity. Social workers are charged with advocating the rights and needs of clients and promoting culturally competent practice (see National Association of Social Workers, 1996, 2003). In our work, at all levels and systems, we are obligated to identify human rights concerns, social inequities, instances of oppression, and other forms of injustice.

Oppressive social and economic forces must be acknowledged, and social justice-oriented policies and structures must be promoted in work at the micro, mezzo, and macro levels (Mackelprang & Salsgiver, 1999). The quest for social and economic justice is supported by practice models that engage the strengths perspective and theory of social construction (Devore & Schlesinger, 1998). To achieve justice as the world grows smaller through the process of globalization, the United States will have to change its commitment of resources to support education, health care, retraining, and Social Security/pension funds (Friedman, 2006). Unless we develop compassionate and responsive systems, we will continue to fall further behind in this quest each year.

References

Abt-Perkins, D., Hauschildt, P., & Dale, H. (2000). Becoming multicultural supervisors: Lessons from a collaborative field study. *Journal of Curriculum and Supervision, 16*(1), 28–47.

Acuña, R. F. (2003). *U.S. Latino issues.* Westport, CT: Greenwood Press.

Allen, T. E. (1994). *The invention of the white race: Vol. 1. Racial oppression and social control.* New York: Verso.

Anthias, F. (2001). The material and symbolic in theorizing social stratification: Issues of gender, ethnicity and class. *British Journal of Sociology, 52*(3), 367–390.

Appleby, G. A., Colon, E., & Hamilton, J. (2001). *Diversity, oppression and social functioning: Person in environment assessment and intervention.* Boston: Allyn & Bacon.

Baines, D. (2000). Everyday practices of race, class and gender: Struggles, skills, and radical social work. *Journal of Progressive Human Services, 11*(2), 5–27.

Bambara, T. C. (1981). Foreword. In C. Moraga & G. Anzaldua (Eds.), *This bridge called my back: Writings by radical women of color* (pp. v–vii). Watertown, MA: Persephone Press.

Banks, J. A. (1997). *Educating citizens in a multicultural society.* New York: Teachers College Press.

Barnes, C. (1991). *Disabled people in Britain and discrimination.* London: Hurst.

Barnes, C., & Mercer, G. (2003). *Disability.* Cambridge, MA: Polity Press.

Baron, J. N., Grusky, D. B., & Treiman, D. J. (1996). Social differentiation and inequality: Some reflections on the state of the field. In J. N. Baron, D. B. Grusky, & D. J. Treiman (Eds.), *Social differentiation and social inequality: Essays in honor of John Pock* (pp. 345–365). Boulder, CO: Westview Press.

Bartlett, J. (1992). *Bartlett's familiar quotations* (16th ed.). Boston: Little, Brown.

Bascara, V. (2001). *Model-minority imperialism.* Minneapolis: University of Minnesota Press.

Bauman, J. (2005). *How changing ads in health and fitness can change attitudes.* Retrieved December 30, 2007, from http://ncpad.org/yourwrites/fact_sheet.php?sheet=243

Baynton, D. C. (2001). Disability and the justification of inequality in American history. In P. K. Longmore & L. Umansky (Eds.), *The new disability history: American perspectives* (pp. 33–58). New York: New York University Press.

Bean, F. D., Trejo, S. J., Capps, R., & Tyler, M. (2001). *The Latino middle class: Myth, reality, and potential.* Claremont, CA: Thomas Rivera Policy Institute.

Bell, L. A. (1997). Theoretical foundations for social justice education. In M. Adams, L. A. Bell, & P. Griffin (Eds.), *Teaching for diversity and social justice: A sourcebook* (pp. 3–15). New York: Routledge.

Bem, S. (1993). *The lenses of gender.* New Haven, CT: Yale University Press.

Berkman, C. S., & Zinberg, C. (1997). Homophobia and heterosexism in social workers. *Social Work, 42*(4), 319–333.

Bettcher, T. M. (2007). Evil deceivers and make-believers: On transphobic violence and the politics of Illusion. *Hypatia: A Journal of Feminist Philosophy, 22*(3), 43–65.

Bilodeau, B. L., & Renn, K. A. (2005). Analysis of LGBT identity development models and implications for practice. *New Directions for Student Services, 111*, 25–39.

Bivens, D. (1995). *Internalized racism: A definition.* Retrieved January 14, 2008, from http://www.thewtc.org/Internalized_Racism.pdf

Bogdan, R. (1988). *Freak show: Presenting human oddities for amusement and profit.* Chicago: University of Chicago Press.

Boston Women's Health Book Collective. (1998). *Our bodies, ourselves: For the new century.* New York: Touchstone.

Brantlinger, E. (2001). Poverty, class and disability: A historical, social, and political perspective. *Focus on Exceptional Children, 33*(7), 1-19.

Brewer, R. M. (1993). Theorizing race, class and gender: The new scholarship of black feminist intellectuals and black women's labor. In S. M. James & A. P. A. Busia (Eds.), *Theorizing black feminisms: The visionary pragmatism of black women* (pp. 13-30). New York: Routledge.

Brooks, F. (2000). Beneath contempt: The mistreatment of non-traditional/gender atypical boys. *Journal of Gay & Lesbian Social Services, 12*(1/2), 107-115.

Bruining, M. O. (1995a). A few thoughts from a Korean, adopted, lesbian, writer/poet, and social worker. In H. Hidalgo (Ed.), *Lesbians of color: Social and human services* (pp. 61-66). New York: Haworth Press.

Bruining, M. O. (1995b). Whose daughter are you? Exploring identity issues of lesbians who are adopted. In H. Hidalgo (Ed.), *Lesbians of color: Social and human services* (pp. 43-60). New York: Haworth Press.

Bryan, W. (1999). *Multicultural aspects of disability: A guide to understanding and assisting minorities in the rehabilitation process.* Springfield, IL: Charles C. Thomas.

Bryson, V. (1999). *Feminist debates: Issues of theory and political practice.* New York: New York University Press.

Buchanan, P. J. (2002). *The death of the West: How dying populations and immigrant invasions imperil our country and civilization.* New York: Thomas Donne Books.

Burr, V. (1995). *Introduction to social constructionism.* New York: Routledge.

Butler, J. (1999). *Gender trouble: Feminism and the subversion of identity.* New York: Routledge.

Caiazza, A., Shaw, A. & Werschkul, M. (2004). *Women's economic status in the States: Wide disparities by race, ethnicity, and region.* Retrieved January 3, 2008, from http://www.iwpr.org/pdf/R260.pdf

Camarota, S. A. (2003, November). *Immigration in a time of recession: An examination of trends since 2000.* Retrieved August 29, 2007, from http://www.cis.org/articles/2003/back1603.html

Carter, R. T. (1993). Does race or racial identity attitudes influence the counseling process in black and white dyads? In J. E. Helms (Ed.), *Black and white racial identity* (pp. 145-163). Westport, CT: Praeger.

Carter, R. T. (1995). *The influence of race and racial identity in psychotherapy.* New York: John Wiley & Sons.

Center for Disease Control. (n.d.). *American Indian & Alaskan Native (AI/AN) populations.* Retrieved July 15, 2005, from http://www.cdc.gov/omh/Populations/AIAN/AIAN.htm

Center for Immigration Studies. (2001). *Labor market characteristics of Mexican immigrants in the United States.* Retrieved August 29, 2007, from http://www.cis.org/articles/2001/mexico/labor.html

Chae, M. H. (2001/2002). Acculturation conflicts among Asian Americans: Implications for practice. *New Jersey Journal of Professional Counseling, 56,* 24-30.

Chan, K. (2001). To be objectified. In K. K. Kumashiro (Ed.), *Troubling intersections of race and sexuality: Queer students of color and anti-oppressive education* (pp. 33-35). New York: Rowman & Littlefield.

Chernus, I. (2006). *Monsters to destroy: The neoconservative war on terror and sin.* Boulder, CO: Paradigm.

Chestang, L. W. (1972). *Character development in a hostile environment* (Occasional Paper No. 3). Chicago: University of Chicago, School of Social Service Administration.

Chestang, L. W. (1984). Racial and personal identity in the black experience. In B. W. White (Ed.), *Color in a white society* (pp. 83-94). Silver Spring, MD: National Association of Social Workers.

Cohen Konrad, S. (2003). *Transitional experiences for mothers whose children acquire unexpected disabilities: A phenomenological perspective.* Unpublished doctoral dissertation, Simmons College.

Collins, P. H. (1996). What's in a name? Womanism, black feminism, and beyond. *Black Scholar, 26*(1), 9-17.

Collins, C., & Veskel, F. (2004). Economic apartheid in America. In M. L. Andersen & P. H. Collins (Eds.), *Race, class, and gender: An anthology* (5th ed., pp. 127-165). New York: Thomson/Wadsworth.

Cook, E. P. (1985). *Psychological androgyny.* New York: Pergamon Press.

Corbett, K. (1999). Homosexual boyhood: Notes on girlboys. In M. Rottnek (Ed.), *Sissies and tomboys: Gender nonconformity and homosexual childhood* (pp. 107-139). New York: New York University Press.

Council on Social Work Education. (2003). *Handbook on accreditation standards and procedures* (5th ed.). Alexandria, VA: Author.

Cramer, E. P., & Gilson, S. F. (1999). Queers and crips: Parallel identity development processes for persons with nonvisible disabilities and lesbian, gay, and bisexual persons. *International Journal of Sexuality and Gender Studies, 4*(1), 1566-1768.

Cranny-Francis, A., Waring, W., Stauropoulos, P., & Kirby, J. (2003). *Gender studies: Terms and debates.* New York: Palgrave Macmillan.

Crenshaw, K. (1990). A black feminist critique of antidiscrimination law and politics. In D. Kairys (Ed.), *The politics of law: A progressive critique* (pp. 195-218). New York: Pantheon Books.

Crenshaw, K. (1995). Mapping the margins: Intersectionality, identity politics, and violence against women of color. In K. Crenshaw, N. Gotanda, G. Peller, & K. Thomas (Eds.), *Critical race theory: The key writings that formed the movement* (pp. 357-384). New York: New Press.

Cross, W. E. (1978). The Cross and Thomas models of psychological Nigrescence. *Journal of Black Psychology, 5*, 13-19.

Cross, W. E. (1980). *Models of psychological Nigrescence: A literature review.* In R. L. Jones (Ed.), *Black psychology* (2nd ed., pp. 81-89). New York: Harper & Row.

Cross, W. E. (1991). *Shades of black: Diversity in African-American identity.* Philadelphia, PA: Temple University Press.

Cuomo, C. (2003). *The philosopher queen: Feminist essays on war, love and knowledge.* Lanham, MD: Rowman & Littlefield.

Currah, P., & Minter, S. (2000). *Transgender equality: A handbook for activists and policymakers.* Washington, DC: National Gay and Lesbian Task Force.

Curry-Stevens, A. (2005, May). *Pedagogy for the privileged: Transformation processes and ethical dilemmas.* Paper delivered at the twenty-fourth annual conference of the Canadian Association for the Study of Adult Education, London, Ontario. Retrieved September 3, 2007, from http://www.oise.utoronto.ca/CASAE/cnf2005/2005onlineProceedings/CAS2005Pro-Curry-Stevens.pdf

Dalton, H. (2002). Failing to see. In P. Rothenberg (Ed.), *White privilege: Essential readings on the other side of racism* (pp. 15-18). New York: Worth.

Daniel, R. G. (2002). *More than black: Multiracial identity and the new racial order.* Philadelphia, PA: Temple University Press.

Davis, K., Moore, W., & Tumin, T. (2006). *Some principles of stratification.* Retrieved December 13, 2006, from http://www.soc.iastate.edu/sapp/DavisMoore.html

Dawson, M. C. (2001). *Black visions: The roots of contemporary African-American political ideologies.* Chicago: University of Chicago Press.

Delgado, R., & Stefancic, J. (2001). *Critical race theory.* New York: New York University Press.

Denmark, F., Eisberg, K., Heitner, E., & Holder, N. (2003). Immigration to the United States: The dream and the reality. In L. Adler & U. Gielen (Eds.), *Migration: Immigration and emigration in international perspective* (pp. 73-104). Westport, CT: Praeger.

Devore, W., & Schlesinger, E. G. (1998). *Ethnic-sensitive social work practice* (5th ed.). Boston: Allyn & Bacon.

Dixon, D. (2006, March). *Migration Policy Institute: Characteristics of the Asian born in the United States.* Retrieved July 2, 2007, from http://www.migrationinformation.org/USfocus/display.cfm?ID=378

Domestic Workers United & DataCenter. (2006). *Home is where the work is: Inside New York's domestic work industry.* Retrieved December 24, 2007, from http://www.datacenter.org/reports/homeiswheretheworkis.pdf

Downing, N. E., & Roush, K. L. (1985). From passive acceptance to active commitment: A model of feminist identity development for women. *Counseling Psychologist, 13*(4), 695-709.

Duany, J. (2002). *The Puerto Rican nation on the move: Identities on the island and in the United States.* Chapel Hill: University of North Carolina Press.

Echols, A. (1989). *Daring to be bad: Radical feminism in America.* Minneapolis: University of Minnesota Press.

Ehrenreich, B. (2002). Maid to order. In B. Ehrenreich & A. R. Hochschild (Eds.), *Global woman: Nannies, maids, and sex workers in the new economy* (pp. 85-103). New York: Metropolitan Books.

Ehrenreich, B., & Hochschild, A. R. (2002). Introduction. In B. Ehrenreich & A. R. Hochschild (Eds.), *Global woman: Nannies, maids, and sex workers in the new economy* (pp. 1-13). New York: Metropolitan Books.

Eibel, F. (2007). *The American resistance: How many illegal aliens are in the U.S.?* Retrieved July 5, 2007, from http://www.theamericanresistance.com/ref/illegal_alien_numbers.html

Ewalt, P. L. (1994). Poverty matters. *Social Work, 39*(2), 149-151.

Faludi, S. (1991). *Backlash: The undeclared war against American women.* New York: Crown.

Fausto-Sterling, A. (1992). *Myths of gender: Biological theories about women and men.* New York: Basic Books.

Fenton, S. (1999). *Ethnicity: Racism, class and culture.* New York: Rowman & Littlefield.

Ferdman, B. M., & Gallegos, P. I. (2001). Racial identity development and Latinos in the United States. In C. L. Wijeyesinghe & B. W. Jackson III (Eds.), *New perspectives on racial identity development: A theoretical and practical anthology* (pp. 32-66). New York: New York University Press.

Fiscuss, R. J. (1992). *The constitutional logic of affirmative action: Making the case for quotas.* Durham, NC: Duke University Press.

Foner, N. (2003). Introduction. Anthropology and contemporary immigration to the United States: Where we have been and where we are going. In N. Foner (Ed.), *American arrivals: Anthropology engages the new immigration* (pp. 3-44). Santa Fe, NM: School of American Research Press.

Freire, P. (1982). *Pedagogy of the oppressed.* New York: Continuum.

Freire, P. (1991). The importance of the act of reading. In C. Mitchell & K. Weiler (Eds.), *Rewriting literacy: Culture and the discourse of the other* (pp. 139-145). Westport, CT: Bergin & Garvey.

Freire, P. (1993). *Pedagogy of the oppressed.* New York: Continuum.

Freire, P. (1997). *Pedagogy of the heart.* New York: Continuum.

Friedman, T. L. (2006). *The world is flat: A brief history of the twenty-first century.* New York: Farrar, Straus and Giroux.

Frye, M. (2000). Oppression. In P. S. Rothenberg (Ed.), *Race, class, and gender in the United States: An integrated study* (5th ed., pp. 139-142). New York: Worth.

Fuller, S. (2000). Social epistemology as a critical philosophy of multiculturalism. In R. Mahalingan & C. McCarthy (Eds.), *Multicultural curriculum: New directions for social theory, practice, and policy* (pp. 15-37). New York: Routledge.

Gainor, K. A. (2000). Including transgender issues in lesbian, gay, and bisexual psychology: Implications for clinical practice and training. In B. Greene & G. L. Croom (Eds.), *Education, research, and practice in lesbian, gay, bisexual, and transgendered psychology: A resource manual* (pp. 131-160). Thousand Oaks, CA: Sage.

Garbarino, J. (1999). *Lost boys: Why our sons turn violent and how we can save them.* New York: Anchor Books.

Garland, R. (1995). *The eye of the beholder: Deformity and disability in the Greco-Roman world.* Ithaca: Cornell University Press.

Garnets, L. D. (2002). Sexual orientations in perspective. *Cultural Diversity and Ethnic Minority Psychology, 8*(2), 115-129.

Garnets, L. D., & Peplau, L. A. (2001). A new paradigm for women's sexual orientation: Implications for therapy. *Women & Therapy, 24*(1/2), 111-121.

Garrett, M. (2001). Eres Maricon? Por "Eladio." In K. K. Kumashiro (Ed.), *Troubling intersections of race and sexuality: Queer students of color and anti-oppressive education* (pp. 33-35). New York: Rowman & Littlefield.

Gil, D. G. (1998). *Confronting injustice and oppression: Concepts and strategies for social workers.* New York: Columbia University Press.

Gilbert, D. (2002). *The American class structure in an age of growing inequality.* Belmont, CA: Wadsworth.

Giroux, H. A. (1993). Literacy and the politics of difference. In C. Lankshear & P. L. McLaren (Eds.), *Critical literacy: Politics, praxis, and the postmodern* (pp. 367-378). Albany: State University of New York.

Giroux, H. A. (1994). Living dangerously: Identity politics and the new cultural racism. In H. A. Giroux & P. McLaren (Eds.), *Between borders: Pedagogy and the politics of cultural studies* (pp. 29-56). New York: Routledge.

Giroux, H. A. (1997). *Pedagogy and the politics of hope: Theory, culture, and schooling.* Boulder, CO: Westview Press.

Glazer, N. (1997). *We are all multiculturalists now.* London: Harvard University Press.

Glenn, E. N. (1992). From servitude to service work: Historical continuities in the racial division of paid reproductive labor. *Signs, 18*, 1-43.

Gordon, L. (1983). Why CIBC is dealing with homophobia. *Interracial Books for Children Bulletin, 14*(3/4), 3.

Grant, J. (Ed.). (1995). *Perspectives on womanist theology.* Atlanta, GA: ITC Press.

Greene, B. (2000). Beyond heterosexism and across the cultural divide: Developing an inclusive lesbian, gay, and bisexual psychology: A look to the future. In B. Greene & G. L. Croom (Eds.), *Education, research, and practice in lesbian, gay, bisexual, and transgendered psychology: A resource manual* (pp. 1-45). Thousand Oaks, CA: Sage.

Guralnik, J. M., & Simonsick, E. M. (1993). Physical disability in older Americans. *Journal of Gerontology, 48*, 3-16.

Hahn, H. (1987). Civil rights for disabled Americans: The foundation for a political agenda. In A. Gertner & T. Joe (Eds.), *Images of the disabled, disabling images* (pp. 181-203). New York: Praeger.

Hancock, K. A. (2000). Lesbian, gay, and bisexual lives: Basic issues in psychotherapy training and practice. In B. Greene & G. L. Croom (Eds.), *Education, research, and practice in lesbian, gay, bisexual, and transgendered psychology: A resource manual* (pp. 91-130). Thousand Oaks, CA: Sage.

Handrahan, L. (2002). *Gendering ethnicity.* New York: Taylor & Francis.

Hardiman, R., & Jackson, B. W. (1997). Conceptual foundations for social justice courses. In M. Adams, L. A. Bell, & P. Griffin (Eds.), *Teaching for diversity and social justice: A sourcebook* (pp. 30-43). New York: Routledge.

Healey, J. F. (2003). *Race, ethnicity, gender, and class: The sociology of group conflict and change* (3rd ed.). Thousand Oaks, CA: Pine Forge Press.

Helms, J. E. (1984). Toward an explanation of the influence of race in the counseling process: A black-white model. *Counseling Psychologist, 12*, 153-165.

Helms, J. E. (1993a). Applying the interaction model to social dyads. In J. E. Helms (Ed.), *Black and white racial identity* (pp. 177-185). Westport, CT: Praeger.

Helms, J. E. (1993b). The beginnings of a diagnostic model of racial identity. In J. E. Helms (Ed.), *Black and white racial identity* (pp. 83-104). Westport, CT: Praeger.

Helms, J. E. (Ed.). (1993c). *Black and white racial identity.* Westport, CT: Praeger.

Helms, J. E. (1993d). Toward a model of white racial identity development. In J. E. Helms (Ed.), *Black and white racial identity* (pp. 49-66). Westport, CT: Praeger.

Helms, J. E. (1994). Racial identity and racial constructs. In E. J. Trickett, R. Watts, & D. Birman (Eds.), *Human diversity* (pp. 285-311). San Francisco, CA: Jossey-Bass.

Helms, J. E. (1995). An update of Helms's white and people of color racial identity models. In J. G. Ponterotto, J. M. Cases, L. A. Suzuki, & C. M. Alexander (Eds.), *Handbook of multicultural counseling* (pp. 181-198). Thousand Oaks, CA: Sage.

Herek, G. M. (Ed.). (1998). *Stigma and sexual orientation: Understanding prejudice against lesbians, gay men, and bisexuals.* Thousand Oaks, CA: Sage.

Hidalgo, H. (1995). Introduction: Lesbians of color—a kaleidoscope. In H. Hidalgo (Ed.), *Lesbians of color: Social and human services* (pp. 1-5). New York: Haworth Press.

Hochschild, A. R. (2002). Love and gold. In B. Ehrenreich & A. R. Hochschild (Eds.), *Global woman: Nannies, maids, and sex workers in the new economy* (pp. 15-30). New York: Metropolitan Books.

Hoffman, R. M. (2006). Gender self-definition and gender self-acceptance in women: Intersections with feminist, womanist, and ethnic identities. *Journal of Counseling and Development, 84,* 358-372.

Holland, T. P., & Kilpatrick, A. C. (1993). Using narrative techniques to enhance multicultural practice. *Journal of Social Work Education, 29*(3), 302-308.

Hollinger, D. A. (2003). Amalgamation and hypodescent: The question of ethnoracial mixture in the history of the United States. *American Historical Review, 108*(5), 1363-1390.

Hondagneu-Sotelo, P. (2001). *Domestica.* Berkeley and Los Angeles: University of California Press.

hooks, b. (1984). *Feminist theory from margin to center.* Boston: South End Press.

hooks, b. (1994). *Teaching to transgress: Education as the practice of freedom.* London: Routledge.

hooks, b. (1995). *Killing rage: Ending racism.* New York: Henry Holt.

Horse, P. G. (2001). Reflections on American Indian identity. In C. L. Wijeyesinghe & B. W. Jackson III (Eds.), *New perspectives on racial identity development: A theoretical and practical anthology* (pp. 91-107). New York: New York University Press.

Hunter, S. (2005). *Midlife and older LGBT adults: Knowledge and affirmative practice for the social services.* New York: Haworth Press.

Ignatiev, N. (1995). *How the Irish became white.* New York: Routledge.

India, J. X. (2006). *Targeting immigrants: Government, technology, and ethics.* Malden, MA: Blackwell.

Jenkins, S. (1988). Ethnicity: Theory base and practice link. In C. Jacobs & D. Bowles (Eds.), *Ethnicity and race: Critical concepts in social work* (pp. 140-152). Silver Springs, MD: National Association of Social Workers.

Jenson, R. (1998). Men's lives and feminist theory. In K. Conway-Turner, S. Cherrin, J. Schiffman, & K. D. Turkel (Eds.), *Women's studies in transition: The pursuit of interdisciplinarity* (pp. 19-33). Cranbury, NJ: Associated University Presses.

Jivanjee, P. (1999). Empowerment and collaboration with single parents of children with disabilities. In C. L. Schmitz & S. S. Tebb (Eds.), *Diversity in single-parent families: Working from strength* (pp. 181-213). Chicago: Lyceum Books.

Johnson, H. P. (2006). Illegal immigration. *At issue: Public Policy Institute of California.* Retrieved July 2, 2007, from http://www.ppic.org/main/publication.asp?i=676

Johnston, L. (2002). Conquering heterosexism: The gay and lesbian challenge to social work education. *Journal of Baccalaureate Social Work, 8*(1), 1-15.

Kahn, S. (1991). *Organizing: A guide for grassroots leaders* (Rev. ed.). Washington, DC: NASW Press.

Kanpol, B. (1997). *Issues and trends in critical pedagogy.* Cresskill, NJ: Hampton Press.

Kich, G. K. (1992). The developmental process of asserting a biracial, bicultural identity. In M. P. P. Root (Ed.), *Racially mixed people in America* (pp. 263-276). Thousand Oaks, CA: Sage.

Kim, J. (2001). Asian American identity development theory. In C. L. Wijeyesinghe & B. W. Jackson III (Eds.), *New perspectives on racial identity development: A theoretical and practical anthology* (pp. 67-90). New York: New York University Press.

Kincheloe, J., & Steinberg, S. R. (1997). *Changing multiculturalism.* Philadelphia, PA: Open University Press.

King, M. L., Jr. (1990). Letter from a Birmingham jail. In A. O'Gorman (Ed.), *The universe bends toward justice: A reader on Christian nonviolence in the U.S.* (pp. 171-184). Philadelphia, PA: New Society Publishers.

Kondrat, M. E. (1999). Who is the "self" in self-aware: Professional self-awareness from a critical theory perspective. *Social Service Review, 73*(4), 451-477.

Korrol, V. (1996). *The origins and evolution of Latino history.* Reprinted from *OAH Magazine of History, 10.* Retrieved July 16, 2005, from http://www.oah.org/pubs/magazine/latinos/Korrol.Html

Kudlick, C. (2003). Disability history: Why we need another "other." *American Historical Review, 108*(3), 763-793.

Kulis, S., Napoli, M., & Marsiglia, F. F. (2002). Ethnic pride, biculturalism, and drug use norms of urban American Indian adolescents. *Social Work Research, 26*(2), 101-112.

Kumashiro, K. K. (2001). Queer students of color and antiracist, antiheterosexist education: Paradoxes of identity and activism. In K. K. Kumashiro (Ed.), *Troubling intersections of race and sexuality: Queer students of color and anti-oppressive education* (pp. 33-35). New York: Rowman & Littlefield.

Lafromboise, T., Coleman, H. L. K., & Gerton, J. (1993). Psychological impact of biculturalism: Evidence and theory. *Psychological Bulletin, 114*(3), 395-412.

Leigh, J. W. (1998). *Communicating for cultural competence.* Prospect Heights, IL: Waveland Press.

Leistyna, P. (1999). *Presence of mind: Education and politics of deception.* Boulder, CO: Westview Press.

Levine, R. A. (2003). *Assimilating immigrants: Why America can and France cannot.* Santa Monica, CA: Rand.

Lie, G.-Y., & Lowery, C. T. (2003). Cultural competence with women of color. In D. Lum (Ed.), *Culturally competent practice: A framework for understanding diverse groups and justice issues* (2nd ed., pp. 282-309). Pacific Grove, CA: Brooks/Cole.

Linton, S. (1998). *Claiming disability: Knowledge and identity.* New York: New York University Press.

Liu, W. M., Soleck, G., Hopps, J., Dunston, K., & Pickett, T., Jr. (2004). A new framework to understand social class in counseling: The social class worldview model and modern classism theory. *Journal of Multicultural Counseling and Development, 32*(2), 95-123.

Lombardi, E., & Bettcher, T. (2005). Lesbian, gay, bisexual, and transgender/transsexual individuals. In B. Levy & V. Sidel (Eds.), *Social injustice and public health* (pp. 130-144). New York: Oxford University Press.

Long, C. R., & Nelson, K. (1999). Honoring diversity: The reliability, validity, and utility of a scale to measure Native American resiliency. In H. N. Weaver (Ed.), *Voices of First Nations people: Human services considerations* (pp. 91-107). New York: Haworth Press.

Lopez, I. F. (1996). *White by law: The legal construction of race.* New York: New York University Press.

Lorde, A. (1983). There is no hierarchy of oppressions. *Interracial Books for Children Bulletin, 14*(3/4), 9.

Lorde, A. (1984). *Sister outsider: Essays and speeches.* Freedom, CA: Crossing Press.

Loseke, D. R., & Best, J. (Eds.). (2003). *Social problems: Constructionist readings.* New York: Aldine de Gruyter.

Luey, H. S., Glass, L., & Elliott, H. (1995). Hard-of-hearing or deaf: Issues of ears, language, culture, and identity. *Social Work, 40*(2), 177-182.

Lum, D. (Ed.). (2003). *Culturally competent practice: A framework for understanding diverse groups and justice issues* (2nd ed.). Pacific Grove, CA: Brooks/Cole.

Lyman, R. (2006, June 7). Reports reveal Katrina's impact on population. *New York Times.* Retrieved July 6, 2006, from http://www.nytimes.com/2006/06/07/us/nationalspecial/07census.html?_r=1&oref=slogin

Mackelprang, R., & Salsgiver, R. (1999). *Disability: A diversity model approach in human service practice.* Pacific Grove, CA: Brooks/Cole.

Maguire, P. (1987). *Doing participatory research: A feminist approach.* Amherst, MA: Center for International Education.

Maher, F. A., & Tetreatult, M. K. (1993). Frames of positionality: Constructing meaningful dialogues about gender and race. *Anthropological Quarterly, 66*(3), 118-127.

Mallon, G. P. (1999a). A call for organizational trans-formation. *Journal of Gay and Lesbian Social Services, 10*(3/4), 131-142.

Mallon, G. P. (1999b). Knowledge for practice with transgendered persons. *Journal of Gay and Lesbian Social Services, 10*(3/4), 1-18.

Mallon, G. P. (1999c). Practice with transgendered children. *Journal of Gay and Lesbian Social Services, 10*(3/4), 49-64.

Mantsios, G. (2004). Class in America—2003. In P. Rothenberg (Ed.), *Race, class, and gender in the United States: An integrated study* (6th ed., pp. 193-223). New York: Worth.

Marger, M. N. (1997). *Race and ethnic relations: American and global perspectives*. Belmont, CA: Wadsworth.

Marsh, J. C. (2004). Social work in a multicultural society. *Social Work, 49*(1), 5-6.

McLaren, P. (1997). *Revolutionary multiculturalism: Pedagogies of dissent for the new millennium*. Boulder, CO: Westview Press.

McIntosh, P. (1990). White privilege: Unpacking the invisible knapsack. *Independent School, 49*(2), 31-36.

McMillen, J. C. (1999). Better for it: How people benefit from adversity. *Social Work, 44*(5), 455-468.

McPhatter, A. R. (1997). Cultural competence in child welfare: What is it? How do we achieve it? What happens without it? *Child Welfare, 76*(1), 255-278.

McPhatter, A. R., & Ganaway, T. L. (2003). Beyond the rhetoric: Strategies for implementing culturally effective practice with children, families, and communities. *Child Welfare, 82*(2), 103-125.

Mexicans Spreading Out. (2005). *Rural Migration News, 12*(2). Retrieved February 17, 2006, from http://migration.ucdavis.edu/rmn/comments.php?id=997_0_2_0

Meyer, J. W. (1994). The evolution of modern stratification systems. In D. B. Grusky (Ed.), *Social stratification: Class, race, and gender in sociological perspective* (pp. 730-737). Boulder, CO: Westview Press.

Michalko, R. (2002). *The difference that disability makes*. Philadelphia, PA: Temple University Press.

Milkie, M. A. (2002). Contested images of femininity: An analysis of cultural gatekeepers and struggles with the "real girl" critique. *Gender and Society, 16*(6), 839-859.

Miller, D. B., & MacIntosh, R. (1999). Promoting resilience in urban African American adolescents: Racial socialization and identity. *Social Work Research, 23*(3), 159-170.

Moi, T. (1999). *What is a woman? And other essays*. New York: Oxford University Press.

Moradi, B. (2005). Advancing womanist identity development. *Counseling Psychologist, 33*, 225-253.

Mullaly, B. (2002). *Challenging oppression: A critical social work approach*. Toronto, ON: Oxford University Press.

National Association of Social Workers. (1996). *Code of ethics of the National Association of Social Workers*. Washington, DC: Author.

National Association of Social Workers. (2001). *NASW standards for cultural competence in social work practice*. Washington, DC: Author.

National Association of Social Workers. (2003). *Social work speaks: NASW policy statements*. Washington, DC: Author.

Ngan-ling, E. (1996). Introduction. Transforming knowledge: Race, class, and gender. In E. N. Chow, D. Wilkinson, & M. B. Zinn (Eds.), *Race, class, and gender: Common bonds, different voices* (pp. ix-xix). Thousand Oaks, CA: Sage.

Northway, R. (1997). Disability and oppression: Some implications for nurses and nursing. *Journal of Advanced Nursing, 26*, 736-743.

Oliver, M. (1996). *Understanding disability: From theory to practice*. New York: St. Martin's Press.

Omi, M., & Winnant, H. (1994). Racial formations. In P. S. Rothenberg (Ed.), *Race, class, and gender in the United States: An integrated study* (3rd ed., pp. 13-22). New York: St. Martin's Press.

Outlaw, L. (1996). *On race and philosophy*. New York: Routledge.

Parks, C. A., Hughes, T. L., & Matthews, A. K. (2004). Race/ethnicity and sexual orientation: Intersecting identities. *Cultural Diversity and Ethnic Minority Psychology, 10*(3), 241-254.

Patterson, S. (1953). *Colour and culture in South Africa*. New York: Routledge Press.

Pear, R. (2004). Number of people living in poverty increases in U.S. In P. S. Rothenberg (Ed.), *Race, class, and gender in the United States:An integrated study* (6th ed., pp. 286-288). New York: Worth.

Pearlmutter, S. (1999). Lesbian and gay single-parent families. In C. L. Schmitz & S. S.Tebb (Eds.), *Diversity in single-parent families: Working from strength* (pp. 131-161). Chicago: Lyceum Books.

Pharr, S. (1993). Racist politics and homophobia. *Transformation, 8*(4), 1-7, 10.

Pharr, S. (2000). *Homophobia:A weapon of sexism* (Expanded ed.). Berkeley, CA: Chardon Press.

Pierre, J. (1977). Black immigrants in the United States and the "cultural narratives" of ethnicity. *Global Studies in Culture and Power, 11*(2), 141-170.

Pinderhughes, E. (1989). *Understanding race, ethnicity, and power:The key to efficacy in clinical practice*. New York: Free Press.

Pipher, M. (1994). *Reviving Ophelia: Saving the selves of adolescent girls*. New York: Ballantine Books.

Pollack, W., & Shuster,T. (2000). *Real boys' voices*. New York: Penguin Books.

Poston, W. S. C. (1990). The biracial identity development model: A needed addition. *Journal of Counseling and Development, 69,* 152-155.

Potok,A. (2002). *A matter of dignity: Changing the world of the disabled*. New York: Bantam.

Priestly, M. (2001). Introduction:The global context of disability. In M. Priestly (Ed.), *Disability and the life course: Global perspectives* (pp. 3-15). New York: Cambridge University Press.

Prince, J. (1999). Black single-mothers and the politics of oppression: Efforts to effect change. In C. L. Schmitz & S. S.Tebb (Eds.), *Diversity in single-parent families:Working from strength* (pp. 107-130). Chicago: Lyceum Books.

Pulera, D. J. (2002). *Visible differences:Why race will matter to Americans in the twenty-first century*. New York: Continuum.

Pyles, L. (2006). Toward a post-Katrina framework: Social work as human rights and capabilities. *Journal of Comparative Social Welfare, 22*(1), 79-88.

Reagon, B. J. (2000). Section 3. Coalition. In J. F. Perea, R. Delgado,A. Harris, & S. M. Wildman (Eds.), *Race and races: Cases and resources for a diverse America* (pp. 1104-1109). St. Paul, MN: West Group.

Richardson, L. (2005). Sticks and stones:An exploration of the embodiment of social classism. *Qualitative Inquiry, 11*(4), 485-491.

Riggs, M. (1994). *Awake, arise, and act:A womanist call for black liberation*. Cleveland, OH: Pilgrim Press.

Risman, B. (1998). *Gender vertigo*. New Haven, CT:Yale University Press.

Rodgers, H. (2000). *American poverty in a new era of reform*. New York: M. E. Sharpe.

Roediger, D. R. (1999). *Black on white: Black writers on what it means to be white*. New York: Schocken Books.

Roediger, D. R. (2002). *Colored white:Transcending the racial past*. Berkeley and Los Angeles; University of California Press.

Romo-Carmona, M. (1995). Lesbian Latinas: Organizational efforts to end oppression. In H. Hidalgo (Ed.), *Lesbians of color: Social and human services* (pp. 85-93). New York: Haworth Press.

Rosaldo, R. (1989). *Culture and truth*. Boston: Beacon.

Rothenberg, P. S. (Ed.). (2004). *Race, class, and gender in the United States:An integrated study* (6th ed.). New York:Worth.

Rothman, J. C. (2003). *Social work practice:Across disability*. Boston:Allyn & Bacon.

Roulsone, A. (1998). *Enabling technology: Disabled people, work and new technology*. Philadelphia, PA: Open University Press.

Rudowitz, R., Rowland, D., & Shartzer, A. (2006). Health care in New Orleans before and after Katrina. *Health Affairs, 25*(5), 393-406.

Saleebey, D. (1994). Culture, theory, and narrative: The intersection of meaning in practice. *Social Work, 39*(4), 351-359.

Saleebey, D. (2002). Introduction: Power in the people. In D. Saleebey (Ed.), *The strengths perspective in social work practice* (pp. 1–22). Boston: Allyn & Bacon.

Saulnier, C. F. (2000). Incorporating feminist theory into social work practice: Group work examples. *Social Work with Groups, 23*(1), 5–29.

Saulny, S. (2006, June 21). A legacy of the storm: Depression and suicide. *New York Times.* Retrieved July 6, 2006, from http://www.nytimes.com/2006/06/21/us/21depress.html

Saunders, J. J., & Kashubeck-West, S. (2006). The relations among feminist identity development, gender-role orientation, and psychological well-being in women. *Psychology of Women Quarterly, 30*, 199–211.

Schaller, J., & Lagergren Frieberg, J. (1998). Issues of abuse for women with disabilities and implications for rehabilitation counseling. *Journal of Applied Rehabilitation Counseling, 29*(2), 9–17.

Schmitz, C. L. (1995). Reframing the dialogue on female-headed single parent households. *Affilia, 10*, 426–441.

Schmitz, C. L., Stakeman, C., & Sisneros, J. (2001). Educating professionals for practice in a multicultural society: Understanding oppression and valuing diversity. *Families in Society, 82*(6), 612–622.

Schmitz, C. L., & Tebb, S. S. (1999). The multiple faces and realities of single-parenthood: Support, diversity, and shifting demographic patterns. In C. L. Schmitz & S. S. Tebb (Eds.), *Diversity in single-parent families: Working from strength* (pp. 18–32). Chicago: Lyceum Books.

Schmitz, C. L., Vazquez Jacobus, M., Stakeman, C., Valenzuela, G., & Sprankel, J. (2003). Immigrant and refugee communities: Resiliency, trauma, and social work practice. *Social Thought, 22*(2/3), 135–158.

Schultz, A. (1970). *On phenomenology and social relations* (Helmut R. Wagner, Ed.). Chicago: University of Chicago Press.

Segal, U. A. (2002). *A framework for immigration: Asians in the United States.* New York: Columbia University Press.

Sernau, S. (2001). *Worlds apart: Social inequities in a new century.* Thousand Oaks, CA: Pine Forge Press.

Shipler, D. K. (2004). *The working poor: Invisible in America.* New York: Alfred A. Knopf.

Smedley, A. (2007). *Race in North America: Origins and evolution of a worldview* (3rd ed.). Boulder, CO: Westview Press.

Smith, B. (1983). Homophobia: Why bring it up? *Interracial Books for Children Bulletin, 14*(3/4), 7–8.

Smith, B., & Smith, B. (1983). Across the kitchen table. In C. Moraga & G. Anzaldua (Eds.), *This bridge called my back: Writings by radical women of color* (2nd ed., pp. 113–127). New York: Kitchen Table, Women of Color Press.

Smith, L. T. (1999). *Decolonizing methodologies: Research and indigenous peoples.* New York: Zed Books.

Snyder, S. L., Brueggemann, B. J., & Thomson, R. G. (2002). *Disability studies: Enabling the humanities.* New York: Modern Language Association of America.

Social Security Administration. (2007). *2006 Social Security/SSI factsheet.* Retrieved December 30, 2007, from http://www.ssa.gov/legislation/2006FactSheet.pdf

Sodowsky, G. R., Kwan, K. L., & Pannu, R. (1995). Ethnic identity of Asians in the United States. In J. Ponterotto., J. M. Casa, L. A. Suzuki, & C. M. Alexander (Eds.), *Handbook of multicultural counseling* (pp. 123–154). Thousand Oaks, CA: Sage.

Steinmetz, E. (2006). *Americans with disabilities: 2002.* Current Population Reports, P70-107. Washington, DC: U.S. Census Bureau.

Stiker, H. J. (1999). *A history of disability.* Ann Arbor: University of Michigan Press.

Stroman, D. F. (2003). *The disability rights movement: From deinstitutionalization to self-determination.* New York: University Press of America.

Sue, D. W., Carter, R. T., Casas, J. M., Fouad, N. A., Ivey, A. E., Jensen, M., et al. (1998). *Multicultural counseling competencies: Individual and organizational development.* Thousand Oaks, CA: Sage.

Sue, D., & Sue, D. W. (1993). Ethnic identity: Cultural factors in the psychological development of Asians in America. In D. R. Atkinson, G. Morten, & D. W. Sue (Eds.), *Counseling American minorities: A cross-cultural perspective* (4th ed., pp. 199–210). Madison, WI: Brown & Benchmark.

Sue, D. W., & Sue, D. (1999). *Counseling the culturally different: Theory and practice* (3rd ed.). New York: John Wiley & Sons.

Szegedy-Maszak, M. (2001). The power of gender. *U.S. News & World Report, 130*(22), 52.

Tafoya, T. (1997). Native gay and lesbian issues: The two-spirited. In B. Greene (Ed.), *Ethnic and cultural diversity among lesbians and gay men* (pp. 1–10). Thousand Oaks, CA: Sage.

Takaki, R. (1993). *A different mirror: A history of multicultural America*. Boston: Little, Brown.

Takaki, R. (1994). *From different shores: Perspectives on race and ethnicity in America* (2nd ed.). New York: Oxford University Press.

Tarek, M. (2005). The baby with Down syndrome. *Ain Shams Journal of Obstetrics and Gynecology, 2*, 362–365.

Tatum, B. D. (1994). Teaching white students about racism: The search for white allies and the restoration of hope. *Teachers College Record, 94*(4), 462–476.

Tatum, B. D. (2001). Talking about race, learning about racism: The application of racial identity development theory in the classroom. In E. Cashmore & J. Jennings (Eds.), *Racism: Essential readings* (pp. 311–326). Thousand Oaks, CA: Sage.

Tatum, B. D. (2003). *Why are all the black kids sitting together in the cafeteria?* New York: Basic Books.

Taylor, C. (2002). Beyond empathy: Confronting homophobia in critical education courses. *Journal of Lesbian Studies, 6*(3/4), 219–234.

Thomson, R. G. (Ed.). (1997). *Extraordinary bodies: Figuring physical disability in American culture and literature*. New York: Columbia University Press.

Thomson, R. G. (2001). Seeing the disabled: Visual rhetorics of disability in popular photography. In P. K. Longmore & L. Umansky (Eds.), *The new disability: American perspectives* (pp. 335–374). New York: New York University Press.

Thomson, R. G. (2005). Feminist disability studies. *Signs: Journal of Women in Culture and Society, 30*, 1557–1587.

Tong, B. (2000). *The Chinese Americans*. Westport, CT: Greenwood Press.

Torres, V., & Baxter, M. M. (2004). Reconstructing Latino identity: The influence of cognitive development on the ethnic identity process of Latino students. *Journal of College Student Development, 45*(3), 333–347.

Tully, C. T. (2000). *Lesbians, gays, and the empowerment perspective*. New York: Columbia University Press.

Tumin, M. M. (1953). Some principles of stratification: A critical analysis. *American Sociological Review, 18*(4), 387–394.

Turner, J. H. (1991). *The structure of sociological theory* (5th ed.). Belmont, CA: Wadsworth.

United Nations. (2006). *Some facts about persons with disabilities*. Retrieved January 13, 2008, from http://www.un.org/disabilities/convention/pdfs/factsheet.pdf

U.S. Census Bureau. (2000a). *Adding diversity from abroad: The foreign-born population, 2000*. Retrieved January 13, 2008, from http://www.census.gov/population/pop-profile/2000/chap17.pdf

U.S. Census Bureau. (2000b). *Population profile of the United States (Internet release)*. Retrieved August 29, 2007, from http://www.census.gov/population/www/pop-profile/profile2000.html

U.S. Census Bureau. (2001). *The Native Hawaiian and other Pacific Islander population: 2000*. Retrieved September 2, 2007, from http://www.census.gov/prod/2001pubs/c2kbr01-14.pdf

U.S. Census Bureau. (2002). *Poverty in the United States: 2001*. Washington, DC: U.S. Government Printing Office.

U.S. Census Bureau. (2004a). *Ancestry: 2000*. Retrieved January 2, 2008, from http://www.census.gov/prod/2004pubs/c2kbr-35.pdf

U.S. Census Bureau. (2004b). *We the people: Asians in the United States*. Retrieved September 2, 2007, from http://www.census.gov/prod/2004pubs/censr-17.pdf

U.S. Census Bureau. (2004c). *We the people: Hispanics in the United States.* Retrieved January 2, 2008, from http://www.census.gov/prod/2004pubs/censr-18.pdf.

U.S. Census Bureau. (2005a). *Disability 2005: B18030 (disability status by sex by age by poverty status for the civilian non-institutionalized population 5 years and older).* Retrieved December 30, 2007, from http://www.census.gov/hhes/www/disability/data_title.html

U. S. Census Bureau. (2005b). *Earnings by occupation and education.* Retrieved January 13, 2008, from http://www.census.gov/hhes/www/income/earnings/call2usboth.html

U.S. Census Bureau. (2005c). *Income stable, poverty rate increases, percentage of Americans without health insurance unchanged.* Retrieved September 1, 2007, from http://www.census.gov/Press-Release/www/releases/archives/income_wealth/005647.html

U.S. Census Bureau. (2006a). *The American Indian and Alaska Native population: 2000.* Retrieved September 2, 2007, from http://www.census.gov/prod/2002pubs/c2kbr01-15.pdf

U.S. Census Bureau. (2006b). *Americans with disabilities.* Retrieved December 30, 2007 at http://www.census.gov/hhes/www/disability/sipp/disable02.html

U.S. Census Bureau. (2007). *Income, poverty and health insurance coverage in the United States: 2006.* Washington, DC: Author. Retrieved January 1, 2008, from http://www.census.gov/prod/2007pubs/p60-233.pdf

U.S. Department of Justice. (2005). *American with Disabilities Act 1990.* Retrieved December 30, 2007, from http://www.usdoj.gov/crt/ada/cguide.htm

U.S. Department of Labor. (2005). *Findings from the National Agricultural Workers Survey 2001–2002.* Retrieved January 1, 2008, from http://www.doleta.gov/agworker/report9/naws_rpt9.pdf

U. S. Department of Labor. (2006). *Employed persons by detailed industry, sex, race, and Hispanic or Latino ethnicity.* Retrieved December 30, 2007, from http://www.bls.gov/cps/cpsaat18.pdf

U.S. General Accounting Office. (2003). *Social Security and minorities.* Retrieved December 30, 2007, from http://www.gao.gov/new.items/d03387.pdf

Utter, J. (2000). *American Indians: Answers to today's questions.* Norman: University of Oklahoma Press.

Van Soest, D. (2003). Advancing social and economic justice. In D. Lum (Ed.), *Culturally competent practice: A framework for understanding diverse groups and justice issues* (2nd ed., pp. 345–376). Pacific Grove, CA: Brooks/Cole.

Van Soest, D., Canon, R., & Grant, D. (2000). Using an interactive website to educate about cultural diversity and societal oppression. *Journal of Social Work Education, 36*(3), 463–479.

Van Wormer, K. (1994). A society without poverty: The Norwegian experience. *Social Work, 39,* 324–327.

Walker, B. A. (2003). The color of crime: The case against race-based suspect descriptions. *Columbia Law Review, 103*(3), 662–688.

Waller, M., & Yellow Bird, M. (2002). Strengths of First Nations peoples. In D. Saleebey (Ed.), *The strengths perspective in social work practice* (pp. 48–62). Boston: Allyn & Bacon.

Wallerstein, I. (2000). *The essential Wallerstein.* New York: New Press.

Walters, K. L., Longres, J. F., Han, C.-S., & Icard, L. D. (2003). Cultural competence with gay and lesbian persons of color. In D. Lum (Ed.), *Culturally competent practice: A framework for understanding diverse groups and justice issues* (2nd ed., pp. 310–342). Pacific Grove, CA: Brooks/Cole.

Washington, P. A., & Harris, B. J. (2001). Women of color standpoints: Introduction. *NWSA Journal, 13*(2), 80–83.

Weaver, H. N. (1999). Health concerns for Native American youth: A culturally grounded approach to health promotion. In H. N. Weaver (Ed.), *Voices of First Nations people: Human services considerations* (pp. 127–143). New York: Haworth Press.

Weinman, S. (1984). *The politics of human services: Radical alternatives to the welfare state.* Boston: South End Press.

Weinstein, B. (2002, Summer). Understanding presbycusis: Age-related hearing loss. *Age & Vision Newsletter.* Retrieved January 3, 2008, from http://www.lighthouse.org/education-services/professional-education/patient-management/patient-management-dual-sensory-loss/presbycusis

White, F. E. (2001). *Dark continent of our bodies: Black feminism and the politics of respectability*. Philadelphia, PA: Temple University Press.

Wijeyesinghe, C. L. (2001). Racial identity in multiracial people: An alternative paradigm. In C. L. Wijeyesinghe & B. W. Jackson III (Eds.), *New perspectives on racial identity development: A theoretical and practical anthology* (pp. 129-152). New York: New York University Press.

Wildman, S. M., & Davis, A. D. (2002). Making systems of privilege visible. In P. Rothenberg (Ed.), *White privilege essential readings on the other side of racism* (pp. 85-95). New York: Worth.

Willis, E. (1984). Radical feminism and feminist radicalism. In S. Sayers, A. Stephenson, S. Aronowitz, & F. Jameson (Eds.), *The 60's without apology* (pp. 91-118). Minneapolis: University of Minnesota Press.

Wilson, A. (1996). How we find ourselves: Identity development and two-spirit people. *Harvard Educational Review, 66*(2), 303-317.

Wilson, J. C., & Lewieki-Wilson, C. (2001). Disability, rhetoric, and the body. In J. C. Wilson & C. Lewieki-Wilson (Eds.), *Disability in language and culture* (pp. 1-24). Carbondale: Southern Illinois University Press.

Woods, J. M., & Lewis, H. (2005, October 27). *On the aftermath of Hurricane Katrina*. Statement prepared for the Hearings of the United Nations Special Rapporteur on Extreme Poverty.

World march of women in the year 2000—Fight poverty! End violence against women! (2000, March 8). *The Guardian*. Retrieved September 3, 2007, from http://www.geocities.com/cpa_blacktown/20000311iwdayguard.htm

Wren, B. (2000). Early physical intervention for young people with atypical gender identity development. *Clinical Child Psychology and Psychiatry, 5*(2), 220-231.

Yeh, C., & Huang, K. (1996). The collectivistic nature of ethnic identity development among Asian American college students. *Adolescence, 31*, 645-661.

Young, I. M. (1990). *Justice and the politics of difference*. Princeton, NJ: Princeton University Press.

Young, I. M. (2000). Difference as a resource for democratic communication. In A. Anton, M. Fisk, & N. Holstrum (Eds.), *Not for sale* (pp. 109-131), Boulder, CO: Westview Press.

Zinn, H. (2003). *A people's history of the United States: 1492-present*. New York: Perennial Classics.

Zola, I. K. (1993). Self, identity and the naming question: Reflections on the language of disability. *Social Science and Medicine, 36*(2), 167-173.

Index